CAMPAIGN 394

OPERATION *PEDESTAL* 1942

The Battle for Malta's Lifeline

ANGUS KONSTAM

ILLUSTRATED BY GRAHAM TURNER

Series editor Nikolai Bogdanovic

OSPREY PUBLISHING
Bloomsbury Publishing Plc
Kemp House, Chawley Park, Cumnor Hill, Oxford OX2 9PH, UK
29 Earlsfort Terrace, Dublin 2, Ireland
1385 Broadway, 5th Floor, New York, NY 10018, USA
E-mail: info@ospreypublishing.com
www.ospreypublishing.com

OSPREY is a trademark of Osprey Publishing Ltd

First published in Great Britain in 2023

A catalogue record for this book is available from the British Library.

ISBN: PB 9781472855671; eBook 9781472855640;
ePDF 9781472855657; XML 9781472855664

23 24 25 26 27   10 9 8 7 6 5 4 3 2 1

Maps by Bounford.com
3D BEVs by Paul Kime
Index by Nikolai Bogdanovic
Typeset by PDQ Digital Media Solutions, Bungay, UK
Printed and bound in India by Replika Press Private Ltd.

Osprey Publishing supports the Woodland Trust, the UK's leading woodland conservation charity.

To find out more about our authors and books visit **www.ospreypublishing.com**. Here you will find extracts, author interviews, details of forthcoming events and the option to sign up for our newsletter.

Artist's note

Readers may care to note that the original paintings from which the colour plates in this book were prepared are available for private sale. All reproduction copyright whatsoever is retained by the publishers. All enquiries should be addressed to:

Graham Turner, PO Box 568, Aylesbury, Bucks. HP17 8ZX UK
www.studio88.co.uk

The publishers regret that they can enter into no correspondence upon this matter.

Photographs

The images in this work are from the Stratford Archive, unless otherwise indicated.

List of equivalent ranks

German

Generalfeldmarschall	general field marshal
Generalleutnant	lieutenant-general
Generalmajor	major-general
Generaloberst	colonel-general
Kapitänleutnant	lieutenant
Oberleutnant zur See	junior lieutenant
Oberstleutnant	lieutenant-colonel

Italian

Ammiraglio di Divisione	rear admiral
Capitano di Corvetta	lieutenant-commander
Capitano di Fregata	commander
Capitano di Vascello	captain
Contrammiraglio	commodore
Tenente di Vascello	lieutenant

Key to military symbols

Army Group, Army, Corps, Division, Brigade, Regiment, Battalion, Company/Battery, Platoon, Section, Squad, Infantry, Artillery, Cavalry, Airborne, Unit HQ, Air defence, Air Force, Air mobile, Air transportable, Amphibious, Anti-tank, Armour, Air aviation, Bridging, Engineer, Headquarters, Maintenance, Medical, Missile, Mountain, Navy, Nuclear, biological, chemical, Ordnance, Parachute, Reconnaissance, Signal, Supply, Transport movement, Rocket artillery, Air defence artillery

Key to unit identification

Unit identifier — Parent unit — Commander — (+) with added elements — (–) less elements

Front cover main illustration: The Royal Navy fleet carrier *Indomitable* under attack by Ju 87 Stuka dive-bombers. (Graham Turner)
Title page photograph: An Italian SM.79 torpedo-bomber flies over the sinking remains of one of her victims.

CONTENTS

INTRODUCTION

Since 1940, the island of Malta had been a thorn in the Axis side, as it lay astride the sea route between Italy and its North African colonies. From 1941 the Royal Navy had used it as a base for attacks on Axis convoys. The island, though, relied on its own convoys to survive, and during 1941 these had come under increasingly heavy attack. By mid-1942 food was scarce in Malta, and the fuel, ammunition and spares needed to defend the island were fast running out. Attempts to send supply convoys that summer had been largely unsuccessful, and the situation had become critical. So, the decision was made to send through an especially well-protected convoy in a desperate bid to save the island. This crucial mission was codenamed Operation *Pedestal*.

Fortunately for the Allies, the tide of the naval war had shifted slightly. While the Battle of the Atlantic was still raging, the need for larger surface warships in the North Atlantic had diminished. For the moment, this gave the

Although Malta was bombed from the start of Italy's entry into the war, the real onslaught came after Hitler's directive of late 1941, and the transfer of a Luftwaffe Fliegerkorps to nearby Sicily. Although the principal target of the bombers was the harbour and the island's defences, the civilian population suffered heavy casualties.

Royal Navy the muscle it needed. Warships to escort the convoy of 14 ships were gathered, including no fewer than two battleships, four aircraft carriers, seven cruisers and dozens of destroyers. As a result, Convoy WS.5.21S would be the best-protected Malta convoy of the war.

The convoy left Britain on 2 August 1942, and eight days later it reached Gibraltar, the gateway to the Mediterranean. Then, with its escort formed around it, the convoy pressed on towards Malta. The first attacks came the following day, then continued with little respite for the next three days. This assault by air and sea reached a peak as the convoy passed through the Narrows – the constricted channel between Sicily and Tunisia. During these crucial 48 hours, some 550 Axis aircraft and 21 submarines were thrown at the convoy. On 13 August Axis torpedo boats joined in the assault. The British did what they could to fend off these remorseless attacks, and the presence of the British carriers was a great help. Although losses mounted steadily, the convoy continued doggedly on its way.

Finally, between 13 and 15 August the convoy's surviving merchant ships limped into the Grand Harbour at Valletta, Malta. The cost of this partial success, though, had been extremely high. Nine of the convoy's 14 merchantmen had been sunk during the operation, and most of those still afloat had been damaged. The Royal Navy had lost an aircraft carrier, two cruisers and a destroyer. Axis losses were placed at around 60 aircraft and two submarines. On paper Operation *Pedestal* could be seen as a failure. Grim though this toll was, the sacrifice had been well worth it. In their holds, those merchant ships carried the key to victory in the Mediterranean. Thanks to them the pressure on Malta eased, and it could remain that thorn in the enemy's side. Malta had been saved, and now, using the island as a base, the Allies could begin reversing the tide of war in this vital theatre.

During 1942, Malta was one of the most heavily bombed places in the world. The devastation is captured by this view of the bombed-out remains of the Opera House in Valletta, once one of the main cultural centres of the island.

CHRONOLOGY

1940

10 June	Italy declares war on Britain and France.
11 June	First Italian air attack on Malta.
25 June	First Italian convoy bound for Libya sails from Naples.
9 July	Battle of Calabria (Punta Stilo).
1 November	Fleet Air Arm attack on the Italian battle fleet at Taranto.
27 November	Battle of Cape Spartivento (Teulada).

1941

6–14 January	Operation *Excess*, the first major Malta convoy operation.
27–29 March	Battle of Cape Matapan, a British naval victory.
27 April	Athens falls to the Axis, and Greece is overrun.
20 May–1 June	Operation *Mercury*, the Axis invasion of Crete.
22 June	Commencement of Operation *Barbarossa*, the invasion of the Soviet Union.
22 July	Operation *Substance*, a Malta convoy.
24 September	Operation *Halberd*, a major Malta convoy.
21 October	Force K deployed in Malta.
2 December	Führer Directive 38 is signed, ordering redeployment of a Luftflotte (air fleet) to Sicily.
17 December	First Battle of Sirte.

1942

22 March	Second Battle of Sirte.
12–15 June	Operations *Harpoon* and *Vigorous*.
15 June	Battle of Pantelleria – attack on *Harpoon* convoy by Italian surface group.
29 June	Decision made to launch Operation *Pedestal*.
1–27 July	First Battle of El Alamein. Rommel's advance into Egypt is halted.

Operation *Pedestal*

2 August	*Pedestal* convoy leaves the River Clyde, Scotland.
4 August	*Furious* departs from the Clyde.
8 August	Escorts begin refuelling at Gibraltar.
10 August	The *Pedestal* convoy enters Mediterranean.
10–12 August	MG.3 diversionary operation.
10–14 August	Operation *Ascendant*.
11 August	1215–1445hrs: Operation *Bellows*.
	1315hrs: Carrier *Eagle* is torpedoed and sunk by *U-78*.
	2045hrs: First Axis air attack on the convoy, by 36 aircraft.
	2300hrs: Ammiraglio da Zara sails from Cagliari.
12 August	0024hrs: Destroyer *Wolverine* rams and sinks submarine *Dagabur*.
	0915hrs: Second Axis air attack on convoy, by 20 aircraft.

1215–1345hrs: Third Axis air attack on convoy, by 70 aircraft. Merchant ship *Deucalion* is damaged.

1650hrs: Destroyer *Ithuriel* rams and sinks the Italian submarine *Cobalto*.

1835–1850hrs: Fourth Axis air attack on convoy, by 100 aircraft. Carrier *Indomitable* and destroyer *Foresight* are damaged

1900hrs: Da Zara and Parona's cruiser forces combine off Ustica.

2000hrs: Cruiser *Cairo* is torpedoed and sunk, and *Nigeria* and tanker *Ohio* are damaged by submarine *Axum*.

2030hrs: Fifth Axis air attack on convoy, by 20 aircraft. Merchant ships *Clan Ferguson* and *Empire Hope* are sunk and *Brisbane Star* is damaged.

2111hrs: Cruiser *Kenya* is torpedoed and damaged by submarine *Alagi*.

2130hrs: *Deucalion* is scuttled.

13 August   0040–0230hrs: Initial attacks by Axis motor torpedo boats (MTBs). Merchant ship *Glenorchy* is sunk and *Rochester Castle* is damaged.

0051hrs: Da Zara's sortie is aborted.

0107hrs: Cruiser *Manchester* is torpedoed and crippled by MTBs. She is scuttled at 0315hrs.

0315–0445hrs: Second running battle with MTBs. Merchant ships *Santa Elisa*, *Almeria Lykes* and *Wairangi* are crippled. All will sink later that morning.

0715hrs: *Santa Elisa* is sunk in an air attack.

0800hrs: Sixth Axis air attack on convoy, by 12 aircraft. Merchant ship *Waimarama* is sunk.

0807hrs: Italian cruisers *Bolzano* and *Muzio Attendolo* are torpedoed and damaged by Royal Navy submarine *Unbroken*.

0925–1000hrs: Seventh Axis air attack on convoy, by 65 aircraft. Tanker *Ohio* and merchant ships *Dorset* and *Rochester Castle* are damaged.

0955hrs: Destroyer *Foresight* is scuttled.

1125hrs: Eighth Axis air attack on convoy, by 12 aircraft.

1400hrs: Force X hands the *Pedestal* convoy over to the Malta Escort Force and returns to Gibraltar.

1830hrs: Merchant ships *Rochester Castle*, *Port Chalmers* and *Melbourne Star* enter Malta's Grand Harbour.

1955hrs: Merchant ship *Dorset* is sunk in an air attack.

14 August   1530hrs: The straggling merchant ship *Brisbane Star* enters Grand Harbour.

15 August   0800hrs: The heavily damaged tanker *Ohio* enters Grand Harbour.

1800hrs: Force X reaches Gibraltar. Operation *Pedestal* ends.

3 October–
1 November   Second Battle of El Alamein – a decisive defeat of Axis forces in North Africa.

8–16 November   Operation *Torch*, the Allied landings in French-occupied Morocco and Algeria.

ORIGINS OF THE CAMPAIGN

War came to the Mediterranean in June 1940, a month after Germany launched its invasion of France. With the Low Countries overrun, the British driven back across the Channel and the French armies in full retreat, the Italian leader Benito Mussolini wanted his share of the looming victory. His declaration of war against Britain and France came on the same day the Germans entered Paris. Twelve days later the French signed an armistice. Mussolini considered his alliance with Nazi Germany as a partnership of equals. After all, the Italian armed forces were considered strong enough to impose their will on their enemies in the Mediterranean theatre. The Italian navy, the Regia Marina, was larger than the British Mediterranean fleet, while its powerful air force, the Regia Aeronautica, was second to none in the theatre.

Even the Italian army, poised to invade British-held Egypt, was considered a match for the smaller British force facing it there. Mussolini's strategic gamble, though, failed to take into account several challenges. First, any military success in North Africa depended on supplies shipped there from Italian ports. The problem was, the island of Malta lay astride these sea lanes, and it remained under British control. So, in order to safeguard the supply routes to Libya, Malta had to be subdued. The air raids on the island began within a day of Italy's entry into the war.

The British Admiralty never considered Malta a suitable forward base in a modern war against Italy. Historically, it had been the main base of the Mediterranean Fleet, but it was too vulnerable to air attack, and so the fleet was moved to Alexandria in Egypt. The island's meagre defences had been bolstered slightly, but they were still woefully inadequate. Fortunately, Mussolini was reluctant to invade Malta. Instead, he relied on his air force to neutralize the island, so it no longer posed a threat to his supply convoys.

Still, the Italian bombing of Malta was carried out half-heartedly. Instead, priority was given to military operations in North Africa. The spectacular failure of the subsequent Italian offensive, though, dramatically altered the strategic situation. By early 1941 it was clear that without military support from Germany, Italy was likely to lose the war in the desert. Hitler duly ordered the transfer of German military units to the Mediterranean. The Deutsches Afrika Korps (DAK) commanded by Generalleutnant Erwin Rommel arrived in Libya from February 1941. For Malta, though, a more direct threat was posed by Fliegerkorps X. This corps of over 230 aircraft led by General Hans-Ferdinand Geisler was deployed in Sicily that January.

Prelude to *Pedestal*: the Western Mediterranean, December 1941–July 1942

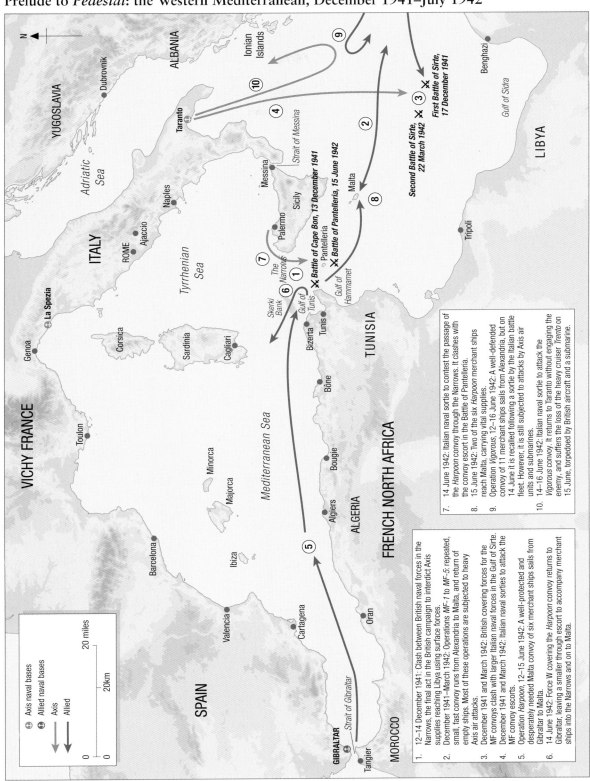

1. 12–14 December 1941: Clash between British naval forces in the Narrows, the final act in the British campaign to interdict Axis supplies reaching Libya using surface forces.
2. December 1941–March 1942: Operations *MF-1* to *MF-5*; repeated, small, fast convoy runs from Alexandria to Malta, and return of empty ships. Most of these operations are subjected to heavy Axis air attacks.
3. December 1941 and March 1942: British covering forces for the MF convoys clash with larger Italian naval forces in the Gulf of Sirte.
4. December 1941 and March 1942: Italian naval sorties to attack the MF convoy escorts.
5. Operation *Harpoon*, 12–15 June 1942: A well-protected and desperately needed Malta convoy of six merchant ships sails from Gibraltar to Malta.
6. 14 June 1942: Force W covering the *Harpoon* convoy returns to Gibraltar, leaving a smaller through escort to accompany merchant ships into the Narrows and on to Malta.
7. 14 June 1942: Italian naval sortie to contest the passage of the *Harpoon* convoy through the Narrows. It clashes with the convoy escort in the Battle of Pantelleria.
8. 15 June 1942: Two of the six *Harpoon* merchant ships reach Malta, carrying vital supplies.
9. Operation *Vigorous*, 12–16 June 1942: A well-defended convoy of 11 merchant ships sails from Alexandria, but on 14 June it is recalled following a sortie by the Italian battle fleet. However, it is still subjected to attacks by Axis air units and submarines.
10. 14–16 June 1942: Italian naval sortie to attack the *Vigorous* convoy. It returns to Taranto without engaging the enemy, and suffers the loss of the heavy cruiser *Trento* on 15 June, torpedoed by British aircraft and a submarine.

A Luftwaffe Ju 88 of Fliegerkorps II, photographed from another aircraft from her squadron. The crews of these twin-engined medium bombers had been specially trained in anti-shipping attacks, and proved much more adept in this role than their Italian counterparts.

Its main job was to protect Rommel's supply lines across the Mediterranean. The Fliegerkorps dominated the waters around Malta until April, when it was sent to Greece to support the German invasion there. It went on to enjoy considerable success against the Royal Navy in the waters around Crete, and ultimately its presence there made it much harder for the British to resupply Malta from the east.

On 24 March Rommel launched an offensive in North Africa that drove the British back to the Egyptian frontier. Tobruk was isolated and besieged, and for the remainder of the year the desert campaign involved repeated British attempts to relieve the port city. Rommel was eventually forced back, but he counter-attacked the following January, driving the British back to the outskirts of Tobruk. In this mobile campaign success depended on plentiful supplies. While the British shipped theirs around Africa, Rommel relied on the sea lanes across the Mediterranean. That was where Malta came in. During 1941, these routes had come under attack from the Malta-based 10th Submarine Flotilla, Force K (a small surface group) and by RAF bombers operating from the island. As a result, Axis convoys suffered heavy losses.

An intial Axis response was the deployment of a U-boat flotilla to the theatre. This achieved some success, most notably the sinking of the carrier *Ark Royal* and the battleship *Barham*. This, though, didn't solve the problem of 'Fortress Malta'. So, in December Hitler signed Führer Directive 38, which ordered a concentration of Luftwaffe forces, combined with the order to bomb Malta into submission. Feldmarschall Albert Kesselring was sent to Italy as Oberbefehlshaber Süd (Commander-in-Chief South), and Generaloberst Bruno Loerzer's Fliegerkorps II was deployed from Russia to Sicily. It would spearhead this bombing offensive. It began in early January 1942, and by April its full impact was being felt. That month, 6,700 tons of bombs were dropped on Malta, the majority on its docks and airfields. More than 1,000 Maltese civilians were killed, and thousands of homes destroyed. However, the most serious problem facing the island's governor Lord Gort was the dwindling stocks of food, water, fuel and ammunition. Without fresh supplies, Malta would eventually be forced to capitulate.

Meanwhile, many of the warships based in Malta were sent away for their safety. The cruiser *Penelope* was so riddled by bomb fragments when she left for Gibraltar that her crew dubbed her 'HMS Pepperpot'. Even the 10th Flotilla was evacuated. Dozens of British aircraft were also lost in the raids. Effectively, Malta had lost her ability to strike at the enemy. Now, she faced a struggle for her very survival. By late May it was clear that a convoy had to reach the island, regardless of the cost. Therefore, the British Admiralty planned to send two seperate relief convoys, approaching the island simultaneously from both east and west.

The western attempt was codenamed Operation *Harpoon*. It involved a fast convoy of six merchantmen, protected by 14 warships, including the anti-aircraft (AA) cruiser *Cairo*. Covering it as far as the Sicilian Narrows

The Italian leader Benito Mussolini inspecting the crew of the battleship *Littorio* in Taranto in 1942. Mussolini was more attuned to the importance of seapower than Hitler, but he was also averse to risking his precious battle fleet. His decision to recall the Italian surface force poised to attack the *Pedestal* convoy was a major miscalculation.

(the strait between Sicily and Tunisia) was Vice Admiral Alban Curteis' Force H, which included two carriers and a battleship. The convoy left Gibraltar on 12 June, and two days later it was subjected to heavy Axis air attacks. That night, Curteis' ships returned to Gibraltar, leaving the convoy and its escort to continue on to Malta. At dawn on 15 June, as it passed the island of Pantelleria, the convoy was attacked by an Italian surface group. In the Battle of Pantelleria that followed, two light cruisers sparred with the escorts, and *Cairo* was damaged. However, the escorts succeeded in protecting the convoy. Instead, it was the Axis bombers which struck the real blows that day, sinking a merchant ship and a destroyer, and damaging the tanker *Kentucky* and another merchantman so badly that they both had to be scuttled. Still, on 16 June the merchantmen *Oriari* and *Troilus* made it into port, despite the loss of another destroyer to enemy mines. *Harpoon* had been a costly undertaking, but at least part of the convoy had made it through to Malta with its desperately needed supplies.

Operation *Vigorous*, the eastern attempt, was notably less successful. This complex operation was devised by Admiral Henry Harwood, Commander-in-Chief of the Mediterranean Fleet, but carried out by his deputy, Rear Admiral Philip Vian. At its heart were the 11 merchant ships sailing in Convoy MW.11. *Vigorous* also involved a deception whereby part of the convoy would make a feint towards Malta, then turn back, in an attempt to lure the Italian battle fleet to sea. Then, when the Italians didn't make contact, they would return to port. That was when Vian would slip through the rest of the convoy. MW.11 was subjected to heavy air attacks, and when the Italians put to sea, they ignored the deception force and headed towards Vian.

On 15 August the convoy reversed course, and while it evaded the Italian fleet, it was repeatedly attacked by Axis bombers and German motor torpedo boats. It was now clear that *Vigorous* was a failure, and so that evening Harwood recalled the convoy. British losses had been heavy: an AA cruiser and three destroyers sunk, and two merchant ships lost. It was clear now that any attempt to reach Malta from the Eastern Mediterranean was doomed to failure. That meant that if Malta was to be saved, the convoy would have to come from the west. Time was also becoming pressing. Malta's governor now reckoned that even with strict rationing, the island would run out of food by 7 September. If a major convoy was to reach the island, it had just seven weeks remaining to make the journey.

OPPOSING COMMANDERS

ALLIES

Throughout Operation *Pedestal*, all decisions lay with the senior commander, Vice Admiral Neville Syfret. He realized that both Prime Minister Winston Churchill and the British Admiralty expected regular progress reports. During *Pedestal*, though, Churchill was in Moscow, so was unable to intervene. Instead, he relied on Syfret's reports forwarded on from London. The admiral and his staff also had to ensure that the Malta garrison was informed of the convoy's progress, so they could organize air cover when it came within range of the island. Ultimately, though, success or failure rested solely in the hands of Syfret and his subordinate Rear Admiral Harold Burrough.

Vice Admiral Neville Syfret (1889–1972) was a South African from Cape Town, and the son of a banker. Syfret joined the Royal Navy when he was 14, and specialized in gunnery. He was a keen cricketer, playing for the Royal Navy in inter-service games. He married in 1913, and five years later his wife Hildegard gave birth to the first of their two sons. By 1914 Lieutenant Syfret was gunnery officer of the light cruiser *Aurora*. He subsequently saw action at Jutland (1916), and ended the war as a lieutenant-commander. Following a staff course in 1924, he became the fleet gunnery officer for the

Mediterranean Fleet, and after promotion to captain, he served in the Admiralty's Tactical Division. His first command came in 1932, when his cruiser *Caradoc* was deployed on the China Station.

Further shore appointments followed, but Syfret returned to sea in 1938, as the captain of the battleships *Ramillies* then *Rodney*. Once war broke out, he was transferred to the Admiralty, becoming Naval Secretary to the First Sea Lord. Promotion to flag rank followed in January 1940, and the following summer he returned to sea, to command the 18th Cruiser Squadron based in Scapa Flow. Then, in early January 1942, Syfret was given the acting rank of vice admiral, a promotion conferred in full the following

Vice Admiral Syfret, a South African, had the unenviable task of fighting the *Pedestal* convoy through to Malta, regardless of the cost. He, though, had planned the operation, and had weighed the risks involved, both to the convoy and to the invaluable capital ships of the escorting force.

Rear Admiral Burrough was given the most challenging job in Operation *Pedestal* – the command of the close escort which would protect the convoy during the passage from the Sicilian Narrows to Malta. His ability to control events was hindered late on 12 August when his flagship *Nigeria* was crippled and he was forced to transfer his flag to a destroyer.

summer. Promotion also brought him command of Force H, the powerful Gibraltar-based naval group. In assuming this command, he took over from the widely respected Vice Admiral James Somerville.

Over the next few months, Syfret led Force H into both the Atlantic and the Western Mediterranean covering various operations. In April 1942 Syfret left for the Indian Ocean, where he supervised the naval side of Operation *Ironclad*, the capture of Madagascar. By then, Force H had been redesignated Force F. When he returned to Gibraltar, Syfret was ordered to plan for a major Malta convoy operation. Inevitably, given his experience and position, Syfret was given full operational command of the *Pedestal* venture. As a result, the task of saving Malta fell on his shoulders.

Syfret was a quiet, unassuming man, and one superior described him as 'perhaps rather shy'. His colleagues spoke very highly of him, though. Admiral Andrew Cunningham, commander of the Mediterranean Fleet described him as a man of great ability, with considerable knowledge and charm, while Admiral John Tovey, commander of the Home Fleet, said Syfret was a clear thinker, and able to make quick decisions. In other words, Syfret might not have been the most dynamic fleet commander of the war, but he was a 'safe pair of hands' – experienced, reliable, intelligent and thoroughly professional. If anyone could push the *Pedestal* convoy through to Malta, it would be Syfret.

Rear Admiral Harold Burrough (1888–1977) was the son of a clergyman from Herefordshire. Burrough was schooled in Oxford, and joined the Royal Navy when he was 15. The young Burrough was prone to seasickness, but did his best to hide this throughout his carreer. Like Syfret, Burrough specialized in naval gunnery, and by 1914 was the gunnery officer of the light cruiser *Southampton*, holding the rank of lieutenant. Burrough saw action at Helgoland Bight (1914), and Jutland (1916) where his cruiser played a prominent role in the battle. Burrough ended the war as a lieutenant-commander. He then served as gunnery officer on the battlecruiser *Australia*, and held a range of sea appointments within the fleet. A spell in the Admiralty was followed by promotion to captain in 1928.

Burrough was given command of the heavy cruiser *London*, followed by two years on the staff of the navy's tactical school, before taking charge of a destroyer flotilla in 1935. From 1937 he served ashore, and when war broke out in 1939, Burrough, a newly promoted rear admiral, was Assistant Chief of the Naval Staff, and the aide de camp of King George V. In October 1941 Burrough was given command of the 10th Cruiser Squadron, flying his flag in the cruiser *Kenya*. He saw action with the Home Fleet, and that same year commanded the naval element of the Vaagso Raid on occupied Norway.

In early June 1942, Burrough and his cruiser squadron were sent to Gibraltar, and named as the *Pedestal* convoy's close escort commander. During *Pedestal*, Burrough's air of calm confidence proved vital to the success of the operation. He was known for his geniality and charm. His actions during the operation were best summed up by his superior, Vice Admiral Syfret, who praised Burrough's steadfastness and resolution. In truth, there was little either Syfret or Burrough could do during those hectic days in the Sicilian Narrows, save from pressing on towards Malta, regardless of the cost.

AXIS

If the British command structure allowed operational decisions to be made by the commander on the spot, the Axis version was much less flexible. This was exacerbated by a lack of cooperation between the Axis partners. At its highest level, Kesselring controlled all German air and ground forces in the Mediterranean Theatre, with the exception of North Africa. Kesselring also had a limited control over the Kriegsmarine; he also held the title of head of the Deutsches Marinekommando Italien (Naval Command, Italy). This though, was merely titular, and operational control was retained by the Kriegsmarine itself. Mussolini retained direct control of his nation's War Ministry, and his decisions guided their actions. In practice, the Regia Aeronautica (Italian Royal Air Force) and the Regia Marina (Italian Royal Navy) operated independently, and inter-service cooperation was poorly coordinated. Still, the allies pooled their intelligence, and agreed broad strategic goals. In the campaign to come, although they might not have known the operational details, both could rely on their ally to play their part.

As the senior Axis commander in the Mediterranean theatre, Feldmarschall Kesselring had to work closely with his Italian allies, but lacked the authority to enforce his plans upon them. Still, they enjoyed reasonably good relations, and so Kesselring was able to make broad operational plans with them – such as a combined response to the *Pedestal* convoy.

The Bavarian-born **Generalfeldmarschall Albert Kesselring (1885–1960)** joined the Imperial German Army shortly before World War I, and served as an artillery officer on both the Eastern and Western fronts, winning the Iron Cross. He served in the Reichsheer after the war, and by 1933 had become an Oberstleutnant. He left the army in 1933 to head the Nazi's nascent Reich Air Ministry. He proved himself a gifted administrator, and rapid advancement in the newly formed *Luftwaffe* followed. In 1936, as a Generalleutnant, he became Chief of Staff of the Luftwaffe, and was an advocate of aerial ground support and accurate bombing. Between 1939 and 1941, Kesselring commanded a Luftflotte during the Polish campaign, as well as during the battles for France and the Low Countries, the Battle of Britain and the invasion of the Soviet Union.

In November 1941, Kesselring was promoted to Generalfeldmarschall, and sent to the Mediterranean. There, he still commanded Luftflotte II, which included Fliegerkorps II and X, but was also

Generaloberst Loerzer, commanding Fliegerkorps II, enjoyed an excellent working relationship with Kesselring, and could be relied upon to produce results. His relations with his Italian counterparts, though, were less amicable, hindered in part by Loerzer's attitude that his air crews should show their allies 'how it was done'.

responsibile for the air campaign against Malta. Known as 'Smiling Albert', Kesselring got on well with both his Italian allies and his own subordinates, but he endured a less amenable relationship with Rommel. Still, Kesselring fully understood the importance of safeguarding the Axis supply routes across the Mediterranean, and the need to subdue Malta. His effectiveness, though, was limited by the constant need to placate his Italian allies, and the distractions of inter-service and departmental rivalry within the German military. However, as a military leader who was able to make the most of his air assets, Kesselring had few rivals.

Generaloberst Bruno Loerzer (1891–1960), a Berliner, joined the Imperial German Army shortly before 1914, at which point he learned to fly, piloting a spotter plane, with Hermann Göring serving as his observer. He subsequently transferred to the Deutsche Luftstreitkräfte (Imperial German Air Service), and duly became one of Germany's leading aces, with 44 kills. After the war he served in the Freikorps, flying in support of it in the struggle for the Baltic States. He went on to support the Nazis, and became leader of their civil flying corps. Loerzer joined the Luftwaffe when it was formed in 1935, and by the start of World War II he had risen to the rank of Generalmajor and was commander of Fliegerkorps II. His Fliegerkorps saw service in France and Russia, where he served under Kesselring. In October 1941 he was transferred to Sicily, where he established his headquarters in Messina. This placed Loerzer at the forefront of the *Pedestal* campaign. Later, he was criticized for the heavy losses within his command – a reflection of Loerzer's demand that his men display aggression during their anti-shipping attacks. A competent rather than an exceptional or inspirational leader, Loerzer could be relied upon to fully commit his command to the air assault on the *Pedestal* convoy.

Generale designato d'Armata Aerea Rino Corso Fougier (1894–1963), a Corsican, was born into a family of Franco-Italian descent. Fougier joined the Italian Army in 1912, and served with distinction during the opening years of World War I. In 1916 he volunteered for the newly formed air force (Corpo Aeronautico Militare), and became a fighter pilot in the Alpine theatre. He ended the war as a squadron leader, with two kills. Fougier remained in service after the war, joining the Regio Aeronautica and steadily rising through its ranks. By 1936, as a Generale di Brigata Aerea, he commanded the Italian air forces in Libya. He went on to command Italian air assets during the Second Italo-Abyssinian War (1935–37) and the Spanish Civil War (1936–39). Then, in 1940, as a Generale di Squadra Aerea, he commanded Italy's contingent during the Battle of Britain. A skilled administrator and aviator, Fougier was popular with his men, and was viewed as a rising star in the air force. In September 1941, when Mussolini sacked the Regio Aeronautica's Chief of Staff Generale d'Armata Francesco Pricolo, Fougier was selected to replace him. That effectively made him the operational head of the Italian air force. Unlike his predecessor, Fougier enjoyed a good relationship with the Germans, particularly Kesselring, although he was still unable to overcome the general distrust between the two allies. Fougier was an advocate of the use of aerial torpedoes, and under his guidance the Regia Aeronautica became a more effective anti-shipping force. During the *Pedestal* campaign he would encourage his subordinates to press home their attacks with aggression.

Generale Fougier, the operational commander of the Regia Aeronautica, was well aware that his air crews were often less proficient than their allies, and so Fougier pressed them to improve their performance by pursuing more aggressive tactics. He was also an advocate of the aerial torpedo, and of new weapons such as the Motobomba running torpedo.

Ammiraglio di Divisione Alberto da Zara (1889–1951) joined the Italian navy at the age of 18, and saw action as a cadet during the brief Italo-Turkish War (1911–12). During World War I he served aboard the destroyer *Ippolito Nievo*. He served in the Aegean, and ended the war as a Tenente di Vascello. During the 1920s he commanded Italian gunboats in the Aegean and the Far East, where he saw further action on the Yangtze River. In 1933 he was promoted to Capitano di Vascello, and in 1935 was given command of the new light cruiser *Duca d'Aosta*. Two years later he was given another new light cruiser, the *Raimondo Montecuccoli*. She served in the Far East until January 1939, and on his return home da Zara was promoted to Contrammiraglio. Soon afterwards he was promoted again, to Ammiraglio di Divisione, and given command of naval forces in Albanian waters.

In June 1940 da Zara was given command of the 4th Cruiser Division. He subsequently participated in the Battle of Calabria (or Punta Stilo). A series of shore-based appointments followed, but in early March 1942 da Zara was appointed as commander of the 7th Cruiser Division, a force of four light cruisers. That June he led them at the Battle of Pantelleria, when he came close to destroying the *Harpoon* convoy. Victory, though, was elusive, largely due to the risk-averse orders he was constrained by. Still, it was a rare success for the Regia Marina, and so in August da Zara was the obvious choice to command an even larger force of cruisers and destroyers, and lead them against the *Pedestal* convoy. Although a skilled and cerebral commander, da Zara was still constrained by a top-heavy command system, which required him to seek approval for virtually any decision he made.

OPPOSITE
Ammiraglio da Zara (right) commanded the Regia Marina's powerful surface group of cruisers and destroyers which was to fall upon the *Pedestal* convoy once it had passed through the Narrows. That made him the man who was in the best position to prevent the convoy from reaching Malta – if he were given his head.

OPPOSING FORCES

ALLIES

Drawing the warships together for Operation *Pedestal* represented a major administrative challenge for the Admiralty. The core of Force Z – the covering force – was made up of three fleet carriers: *Eagle*, *Indomitable* and *Victorious*. *Eagle* was already at Gibraltar, while *Victorious* was in Scapa Flow and *Indomitable* in the Indian Ocean. Rear Admiral Arthur Lumley Lyster commanded the carrier strike force from *Victorious*. A fourth carrier, *Furious*, was also included in the operation, but was there to spearhead Operation *Bellows*, a 'Club Run': the flying-off of fighters to reinforce RAF Malta Command. It, though, would detach from the convoy before it reached the Narrows.

Between them, the carriers embarked 72 Fleet Air Arm (FAA) fighters, in eight squadrons. Some were outdated Fairey Fulmars, but most were the

Like the other carriers of her type, the fleet carrier *Indomitable* had an armoured flight deck, protected by 3in. of steel plate. This was still penetrated by the 250kg SC bombs dropped by the Stukas of Fliegerkorps II on 12 August.

The Illustrious-class fleet carrier *Victorious* was the flag of Rear Admiral Lyster, who commanded the *Pedestal* carriers. Of her 33 embarked aircraft, 21 were fighters. While her Sea Hurricanes were deployed against low-level enemy aircraft, her larger Fairy Fulmars were used to intercept high-level bombers and reconnaissance planes.

far more effective Sea Hurricanes. This caused problems in *Victorious*, as her lifts couldn't handle the new aircraft, so they remained ranged on deck. *Indomitable* also carried a handful of small Martlet fighters (the British version of the Grumman Wildcat), while she, *Victorious* and *Indomitable* also had Fairey Albacore torpedo-bombers – the only strike aircraft in the carrier force.

The threat posed by the Italian battleships led to the inclusion of the battleships *Nelson* and *Rodney* in the covering force, the former also acting as Syfret's flagship. While they only made 21 knots, and so were incapable of pursuing the enemy surface fleet, they had the firepower to counter any Italian battleship.

Also part of Force Z were the Dido-class AA cruisers *Charybdis*, *Phoebe* and *Sirius*, carrying ten 5.25in. guns apiece. Each of these provided dedicated AA protection for a carrier. *Sirius* also carried a Type 281 air-search radar, ideal for detecting approaching low-level attacks.

Surrounding the entire convoy were the escorts. The main body of 13 destroyers and two escort destroyers served under Captain Hutton, the commander of the 19th Destroyer Flotilla. These, together with the carriers, battleships and the three AA cruisers completed Force Z. It would accompany the convoy as far as the Narrows, some ten hours' steaming from Malta, at which point it would return to Gibraltar.

The 10th Cruiser Flotilla formed the core of Force X for *Pedestal*, was made up of the light cruisers *Kenya*, *Nigeria* and *Manchester*. Serving as the close escort, the force was commanded by Burrough, who flew his flag in *Nigeria*. Accompanying him was the older AA cruiser *Cairo*, armed with eight 4in. guns. These were especially useful as both *Nigeria* and *Cairo* were designed as fighter-direction ships, and equipped with powerful air-search radars. This meant they could direct both RAF and FAA fighters in the coming air battle.

A second group of seven destroyers and four escort destroyers was attached to Burrough's Force X. The group would accompany it all the way through to Malta. These escorts were commanded by Captain Onslow of the 6th Destroyer Flotilla.

A further force, Commander Russell's Escort Flotilla drawn from the Western Approaches, was also included as part of Operation *Bellows*, the 'Club Run'. After the Spitfires were flown off from *Furious*, these six destroyers would escort the carrier back to Gibraltar. Another destroyer and escort destroyer would form Force Y. That meant a total of 32 destroyers and escort destroyers were included in the main operation. In addition, the destroyers *Foresight*, *Fury*, *Interpid* and *Icarus* were equipped as minesweepers, and so would lead the way as the convoy passed through the minefield beyond the Narrows.

Four other detached forces also played a part in *Pedestal*. Both Force R from Gibraltar and Force W from Freetown were oiling groups, 'W' consisting of the Royal Fleet Auxilliary (RFA) oiler *Abbeydale* and two corvettes, and 'R' of the RFA oilers *Brown Ranger* and *Dingledale* escorted by four more corvettes. *Abbeydale* was there to replenish the warships as they headed towards Gibraltar, while *Brown Ranger* and *Dingledale* would do the same as the convoy steamed through the Western Mediterranean. Also attached to Force R were the rescue tugs *Jaunty* and *Salvonia*. Their job was to help any ship in distress. While the oilers would return to Gibraltar with Force Z, the intention was that the tugs would accompany Force X on to Malta.

During the run south, the carrier *Argus* would carry out Operation *Berserk*, a series of fighter-direction exercises. *Argus* would then put in to Gibraltar. Finally, to coincide with *Pedestal*, Operation *Ascendant* would involve the departure of the two Operation *Harpoon* merchantmen *Orari* and *Troilus* from Malta, accompanied by Force Y – the destroyer *Matchless*

The *Kenya*, like her sister ship *Nigeria*, was a Colony-class light cruiser, launched in 1940. These were of a more compact design than previous 6in. cruisers like *Manchester*, but essentially they carried the same weaponry, although neither of these Colony-class vessels carried facilities for a seaplane. Their main armament of 12 6in. guns supported by radar made them superior to their Italian counterparts.

and the escort destroyer *Badsworth*. They would slip through the Narrows while the enemy was distracted by the *Pedestal* convoy.

In addition, the 10th Submarine Flotilla, which had recently been re-established in Malta, would act as scouts for the convoy, with two boats stationed off the north coast of Sicily, and six more on patrol between Malta and Pantelleria. Naturally, as well as reconnaissance, they would also be available to attack targets of opportunity – the most important of which was the Italian battle fleet – if it put to sea. Malta was also the source of additional air cover for the convoy. The number of aircraft under Air Vice Marshal Keith Park's command on Malta fluctuated as aircraft were damaged and repaired. Fuel stocks were also a limiting factor. However, in theory he had 136 Spitfires and Beaufighters under his command.

The most important element of all was the convoy itself. The Allies had lost a large number of merchant ships during the war, and fast, modern ones were now hard to come by. This was especially true of tankers. However, it was vital that the convoy should be able to make 16 knots, and so the Admiralty and the Ministry of War Transport worked hard to secure a dozen fast merchant ships. Suitable British tankers weren't available, and so the US Maritime Commission was asked to help. In the end, it took presidential approval to secure the use of the tanker *Ohio*, owned by Texaco. She was duly requisitioned in the Clyde and her American crew replaced by a British one.

Two other American-registered merchant ships took part in the convoy: the *Almeria Lykes* of New Orleans and the *Santa Elisa* of New York. Both retained their American crew, augmented by a small detachment from US naval personnel, to man their AA guns. A detachment of British gunners were also embarked for the voyage. Of the 11 British-registered ships, all but one were fast cargo-passenger liners, most with refrigerated storage facilities. The exception was the *Empire Hope*, a large refrigerated cargo ship owned by the Shaw, Saville & Albion Company. The same company also provided the large cargo-passenger liners *Wairangi* and *Waimarama*. The Blue Star Line's *Brisbane Star* and *Melbourne Star* were similarly sized vessels, while the slightly smaller *Dorset* was supplied by the Federal Steam Navigation Company. Finally, five smaller British-registered ships – the *Clan Ferguson*, *Deucalion*, *Glenorchy*, *Port Chalmers* and *Rochester Castle* – were each owned by other British shipping companies. Before sailing, all of these ships had extra AA armament added, mainly 40mm Bofors and 20mm Oerlikon guns.

AXIS

While the Allied force was primarily naval, the Axis forces facing them predominantly comprised aircraft. In theory, these Axis units coordinated their efforts, but in practice this rarely happened. The Italian Aeronautica Sardegna (Sardinia Air Command) and Aeronautica Sicilia (Sicily Air Command) each consisted of several *Gruppi* (Air Groups), each made up of two or three squadrons. Typical squadron strength was around six to nine aircraft. These *Gruppi* were often combined into a *Stormo* (Air Wing) made up of the same aircraft type.

Numbers fluctuated, but shortly before *Pedestal* there were 73 Italian bombers in Sicily, with another 56 in Sardinia. The majority of these

An Italian SM.79 torpedo-bomber flies over the sinking remains of one of her victims. By this stage of the war, these bombers had largely been converted to carry torpedoes rather than bombs, and during the *Pedestal* operation their air crews proved to be both skilled and courageous.

were Savoia-Marchetti SM.79 Sparviero or SM.84 medium bombers, or German-built but Italian-crewed Ju 87 Stuka dive-bombers. By mid-1942, many of the Savoia-Marchetti medium bombers had been adapted to carry torpedoes. The Aeronautica Sicilia also included a handful of Fiat BR.20 Cigogna bombers. Cover was provided by 47 fighters based in Sicily and another 80 in Sardinia. These were a mixture of Macchi MC.202 Folgore, Fiat G.50 Freccia and Regianno RE.2001 Falco 2 monoplanes, and Fiat CR.42 Falco biplanes.

Officially, Generaloberst Loerzer's Fliegerkorps II, based in Sicily, was part of a larger organization, Luftflotte II – an 'air fleet' commanded by Kesselring himself. However, the Luftflotte included Fliegerkorps X, which remained in Greece throughout the *Pedestal* campaign, as well as Generalmajor Stefan Fröhlich's Fliegerführer Afrika, based in Libya. These, though, would play little part in the *Pedestal* battles. Within Fliegerkorps II the basic operational unit was the *Staffel* (squadron) of nine to 12 aircraft. These were combined into a *Gruppe* (Air Group), usually made up of three to four squadrons. These in turn were grouped together into a *Geschwader* (Air Wing) of three *Gruppen*.

Each air wing was designated by its aircraft type and purpose. Fliegerkorps II included *Kampf* (KG, bomber), *Jagd* (JG, fighter) and *Sturzkampf* (StG, dive-bomber) air wings as well as a *Lehrgeschwader* (LG, Advanced Training Air Wing). Each group within a wing was designated by a Roman numeral (e.g. II./KG 77 for Group II of Bomber Wing 77). Fliegerkorps II also included a night-fighter wing (*Nachtjagdgeschwader*, or NJG) and two squadrons dedicated to reconnaissance (*Aufklärungs*) with the added designation 'F' denoting *fern* (far, or long-range) reconnaissance aircraft. In August 1942 the Fliegerkorps mustered a total of 144 Junkers Ju 88 medium bombers, some of which were adapted to carry torpedoes; 26 Junkers Ju 87 Stuka dive-bombers; six Heinkel He 111 medium bombers used as torpedo-bombers; and 46 fighters, a dozen of which were Messerschmitt Bf 110 night-fighters, and the rest Messerschmitt Me 109Gs. That gave Loerzer a potent force

of 222 combat and reconnaissance aircraft. Most of these were based at airfields in Sicily.

At sea the Axis deployed a patrol line of seven Italian submarines and German U-boats to the north of Algiers, with another 14 boats ready to put to sea. They would also be joined by a third German boat, *U-333*. The Narrows were heavily mined, which prevented the deployment of Italian surface warships there. However, Ammiraglio da Zara's powerful battlegroup of six cruisers was deployed to the north of Sicily, made up of the heavy cruisers *Gorizia*, *Bolzano* and *Trieste*, the light cruisers *Eugenio di Savoia*, *Raimondo Montecuccoli* and *Muzio Attendolo* and 12 destroyers. An equally serious threat was posed by the small MTBs – the Italian Motoscafo Armato Silurante (MAS – Torpedo-Armed Motor Boat) and the slower but larger Motosilurante (MS – Motor Boat), and the German Schnellboot (S-boot – Fast Boat) – known to the Allies as an E-boat. A total of 22 of these vessels were stationed in the area, each armed with two torpedoes.

The Ju 88 twin-engined light bomber was a robust and versatile aircraft and its long range of up to 970nm meant that it could also be used as a long-range reconnaissance aircraft. During *Pedestal* these planes made up the bulk of Fliegerkorps II.

ORDERS OF BATTLE

ALLIES

CONVOY WS.5.21S

14 merchant ships
Convoy Commodore: Commodore A.G. Venables RN rtd.
Almeria Lykes (Captain Henderson), 7,773 tons (Lykes Bros. Steamship Co.)
Brisbane Star (Captain Riley), 12,791 tons (Blue Star Line)
Clan Ferguson (Captain Cossar), 7,347 tons (Scottish Steamship Co.)
Deucalion (Captain Brown), 7,516 tons (Blue Funnel Line)
Dorset (Captain Tuckett), 10,624 tons (Federal Steam Navigation Co.)
Empire Hope (Captain Williams), 12,688 tons (Shaw, Saville & Albion)

Glenorchy (Captain Leslie), 8,982 tons (Glen Line)
Melbourne Star (Captain MacFarlane), 12,806 tons (Blue Star Line)
Ohio (Captain Mason), 9,514 tons (Texaco; oil tanker
Port Chalmers (Captain Pinckey), 8,535 tons (Port Line); commodore's pennant ship
Rochester Castle (Captain Wren), 7,795 tons (Union Castle Line)
Santa Elisa (Captain Thompson), 8,379 tons (Grace Line)
Waimarama (Captain Pearce), 12,843 tons (Shaw, Saville & Albion)
Wairangi (Captain Gordon), 12,400 tons (Shaw, Saville & Albion)

FORCE Z (COVERING FORCE)

Nelson (Captain Jacomb), Nelson-class battleship (flagship, Vice Admiral Syfret)
Rodney (Captain Rivett-Carnac), Nelson-class battleship

Victorious (Captain Bovell), Illustrious-class fleet carrier (flagship, Rear Admiral Lyster)

Indomitable (Captain Troubridge), Indomitable-class fleet carrier (flagship, Rear Admiral Boyd)

Eagle (Captain Mackintosh), Eagle-class fleet carrier

Furious (Captain Bulteel), Furious-class fleet carrier

Phoebe (Captain Frend), Dido-class light AA cruiser

Sirius (Captain Brooking), Dido-class light AA cruiser

Charybdis (Captain Voelcker), Dido-class light AA cruiser

Embarked aircraft

Victorious

16 Fulmar fighters: 809 Naval Air Squadron (NAS) (Lieutenant Savage)/884 NAS (Lieutenant Hallett)

Five Sea Hurricane fighters: 885 NAS (Lieutenant Carver)

12 Albacore torpedo-bombers: 832 NAS (Lieutenant-Commander Lucas)

Indomitable

Five Martlet fighters: 806 NAS (Lieutenant Johnston)

22 Sea Hurricane fighters: 800 NAS (Lieutenant-Commander Bruen)/880 NAS (Lieutenant-Commander Todd)

16 Albacore torpedo-bombers: 827 NAS (Lieutenant-Commander Buchanan-Dunlop)

Eagle

20 Sea Hurricane fighters: 801 NAS (Lieutenant-Commander Brabner)/813 NAS (Lieutenant-Commander Hutchinson)

Furious

Four Albacores: 823 NAS (as spares)

42 Spitfire Mk VB fighters – to reinforce Malta garrison

Attached destroyers: 19th Destroyer Flotilla

Laforey (Captain Hutton), L/M class (flotilla leader)

Lightning (Commander Walters), L/M class

Lookout (Lieutenant-Commander Brown), L/M class

Quentin (Lieutenant-Commander Noble), Q/R class

Somali (Commander Currey), Tribal class

Eskimo (Commander Le Geyt), Tribal class

Tartar (Commander Tyrwhitt), Tribal class

Ithuriel (Lieutenant-Commander Maitland-Makgill-Crichton), mod. G/H/I class

Antelope (Lieutenant-Commander Sinclair), A/B class

Wishart (Commander Scott), mod. V/W class

Vansittart (Lieutenant-Commander Johnston), mod. V/W class

Westcott (Lieutenant-Commander Bockett-Pugh), V/W class

Wrestler (Lieutenant Lacon), V/W class

Wilton (Lieutenant Northey), Hunt class (Type 2) escort destroyer

Zetland (Lieutenant Wilkenson), Hunt class (Type 2) escort destroyer

FORCE X (CLOSE ESCORT)

Nigeria (Captain Paton), Colony-class light cruiser (flagship, Rear Admiral Burrough)

Kenya (Captain Russell), Colony-class light cruiser

Manchester (Captain Drew), Gloucester-class light cruiser

Cairo (Captain Hardy), Carlisle-class light AA cruiser

Attached destroyers: 6th Destroyer Flotilla

Ashanti (Commander Onslow), Tribal class (flotilla leader)

Intrepid (Commander Kitcat); G/H/I class

Icarus (Lieutenant-Commander Maud), G/H/I class

Foresight (Lieutenant-Commander Fell), E/F class

Fury (Lieutenant-Commander Campbell), E/F class

Pathfinder (Commander Gibbs), O/P class

Penn (Lieutenant-Commander Swain), O/P class

Derwent (Commander Wright), Hunt-class (Type 3) escort destroyer

Bramham (Lieutenant Baines), Hunt-class (Type 2) escort destroyer

Bicester (Lieutenant-Commander Bennets), Hunt-class (Type 2) escort destroyer

Ledbury (Lieutenant-Commander Hill), Hunt-class (Type 2) escort destroyer

FORCE R

RFA *Brown Ranger* (Master Ralph), Ranger-class fleet support tanker

RFA *Dingledale* (Master Duthie), Dale-class fleet tanker

Jaunty (Lieutenant-Commander Osburn), Assurance-class rescue tug

Salvonia (Lieutenant Robinson), Salvonia-class rescue tug

Attached corvettes

Jonquil (Lieutenant-Commander Partington), Flower class

Geranium (Lieutenant-Commander Foxall), Flower class

Spiraea (Lieutenant-Commander Miller), Flower class

Coltsfoot (Lieutenant-Commander The Hon W.K. Rous), Flower class

FORCE W

RFA *Abbeydale* (Master Edwards), Abbeydale-class fleet tanker

Attached corvettes

Burdock (Lieutenant-Commander Lynes), Flower class

Armeiria (Lieutenant Todd), Flower class

TEMPORARY ATTACHMENTS

For Operation *Berserk*

Argus (Captain Philip), Argus-class fleet carrier

Embarked aircraft:

Six Sea Hurricane fighters: 804 NAS (Captain Marsh RM)

Force Y escorts

Matchless (Lieutenant-Commander Mowlam), L/M-class destroyer

Badsworth (Lieutenant Gray), Hunt-class (Type 2) escort destroyer

Attached from Western Approaches Command

Keppel (Commander Broome), Shakespeare-class destroyer (flotilla leader)

Malcolm (Commander Russell), Scott-class destroyer

Amazon (Lieutenant-Commander Lord Teynham), Amazon-class destroyer

Venomous (Commander Falcon-Steward), mod. V/W-class destroyer

Wolverine (Lieutenant-Commander Gretton), mod. V/W-class destroyer

Vidette (Lieutenant-Commander Walmsey), V/W class-destroyer

MALTA ESCORT FORCES

17th Minesweeping Flotilla

Speedy (Lieutenant-Commander Jerome) (flotilla leader)

Rye (Lieutenant-Commander Pearson)

Hebe (Lieutenant-Commander Mowatt)

Hythe (Lieutenant-Commander Miller)

3rd Motor Launch Flotilla (seven boats)

ML 121 (Lieutenant-Commander Strowlger) (flotilla leader)

plus *ML-126*, *ML-134*, *ML-134*, *ML-168*, *ML-459*, *ML-462*

OPERATIONAL SUBMARINES IN WESTERN MEDITERRANEAN

10th Submarine Flotilla (Captain Simpson, based in Malta)

(All U-class boats unless noted.)

Safari (Commander Bryant), S class

Unbroken (Lieutenant Mars)

Uproar (Lieutenant Kershaw)

Ultimatum (Lieutenant Harrison)

Unruffled (Lieutenant Stevens)

Utmost (Lieutenant Langridge)

United (Lieutenant Barlow)

Una (Lieutenant Martin)

P-222 (Lieutenant-Commander Mackenzie), S class

ROYAL AIR FORCE, MALTA COMMAND

Air Vice Marshal Sir Keith Park

Fighters

Spitfires: 126 Sqn, 185 Sqn, 229 Sqn, 249 Sqn, 1435 Sqn

Beaufighters: 89 Sqn (night-fighters), 235 Sqn, 248 Sqn, 252 Sqn

FLEET AIR ARM, MALTA COMMAND

27 Albacore torpedo-bombers: 828 NAS (Lieutenant Haynes RAN)

One Swordfish torpedo-bomber, attached from 830 NAS (Captain Ford RM)

AXIS

NAVAL FORCES

3rd Cruiser Division
Gorizia (Capitano di Vascello Melodia), Zara-class heavy cruiser (flagship, Ammiraglio Parona)
Bolzano (Capitano di Vascello Mezzadra), Bolzano-class heavy cruiser
Trieste (Capitano di Vascello Rouselle), Trento-class heavy cruiser

Attached destroyers (10th and 11th Destroyer divisions)
(All Soldati-class vessels unless noted.)
Aviera (Capitano di Vascello Minotti) (flotilla leader)
Geniere (Capitano di Fregata Notarbartolo)
Camicia Nera (Capitano di Fregata Foscari)
Legionario (Capitano di Fregata Tagliamonte)
Ascari (Capitano di Fregata Capone)
Corsaro (Capitano di Fregata Sagamoso)
Grecale (Capitano di Fregata Gasparrini), Maestrale class

7th Cruiser Division
Eugenio di Savoia (Capitano di Vascello Zannoni), D'Aosta-class light cruiser (flagship, Ammiraglio da Zara)
Muzio Attendolo (Capitano di Vascello Schiavuta), Montecuccoli-class light cruiser
Raimondo Montecuccoli (Capitano di Vascello Solari), Montecuccoli-class light cruiser

Attached destroyers (10th and 13th Destroyer divisions)
Maestrale (Capitano di Vascello Pontremoli), Maestrale class (flotilla leader)
Vincenzo Gioberti (Capitano di Fregata Prato), Oriani class
Alfredo Oriani (Capitano di Fregata Pesci), Oriani class
Fuciliere (Capitano di Fregata del Grande), Soldati class

Attached minelaying destroyer
Lanzerotto Malocello (Capitano di Fregata Tona), mod. Navigatore class

Motor Torpedo Boats
3rd S-Boat Flotilla (four S30 Group boats)
   S-58 (Kapitänleutnant Kemnade, flotilla leader), *S-30, S-36, S-59*
2nd MS Division (six MS Type 1 boats)
   MS-16 (Capitano di Corvetta Manuti, division leader), *MS-22, MS-23, MS-25, MS-26, MS-31*
15th MAS Division (four MAS boats) – all MAS-526-type boats unless noted:
   MAS-549 (Tenente di Vascello Giuffra, division leader), *MAS-543, MAS-548, MAS-561* (MAS-555 type)
18th MAS Division (four MAS boats) – all MAS-555-type boats unless noted:
   MAS-553 (MAS-551-type, Tenente di Vascello Paolizza, division leader), *MAS-556, MAS-560, MAS-562*
20th MAS Division (four MAS boats) – all MAS-555-type boats unless noted:
   MAS-552 (Tenente di Vascello Perasso, division leader), *MAS-554* (both MAS-551 types), *MAS-557, MAS-564*

Operational submarines
Italian boats:
Alagi (Tenente di Vascello Puccini), Adua class
Ascianghi (Tenente di Vascello Bombig), Adua class
Asteria (Tenente di Vascello Beltrame), Acciaio class
Avorio (Tenente di Vascello Priggione), Acciaio class
Axum (Tenente di Vascello Ferrini), Adua class
Brin (Tenente di Vascello Andreotti), Brin class
Bronzo (Tenente di Vascello Buldrini), Acciaio class
Cobalto (Tenente di Vascello Amicarelli), Acciaio class
Dagabur (Tenente di Vascello Pecori), Adua class
Dandolo (Tenente di Vascello Campanella), Marcello class
Dessiè (Tenente di Vascello Scandola), Adua class
Emo (Tenente di Vascello Franco), Marcello class
Giada (Tenente di Vascello Cavallina), Acciaio class
Granto (Tenente di Vascello Sposito), Acciaio class
Otaria (Tenente di Vascello Gorini), Glauco class
Uarsciek (Tenente di Vascello Targia), Adua class
Velella (Tenente di Vascello Febbraro), Argo class
Volframio (Tenente di Vascello Manunta), Acciaio class

German boats:
U-73 (Kapitänleutnant Rosenbaum), Type VIIB
U-205 (Kapitänleutnant Rerchke), Type VIIC
U-333 (Kapitänleutnant Cremer), Type VIIC

AIR UNITS

Regia Aeronautica (Italian Air Force)
Sardinia:
28° Stormo (nine CANT Z.1007b Alcione reconnaissance aircraft)
32° Stormo (eight SM.84 medium bombers and 16 SM.84 torpedo-bombers)
130° Gruppo (20 SM.79 Sparviero torpedo-bombers and ten SM.85 dive-bombers)
105° Stormo (12 SM.79 Sparviero torpedo-bombers)
160° Gruppo (16 CR.42 Falco fighters)
153° Gruppo (22 MC.202 Folgore fighters)
2° Gruppo (28 RE.2001 Falco 2 fighters)
24° Gruppo (14 G.50 Freccia fighters)

Sicily:
Assorted commands (11 SM.79 Sparviero and Cr.25 reconnaissance aircraft)
Assorted commands (25 SM.84, SM.79 Sparviero and BR.20 Cigogna bombers)
132° Gruppo (15 SM.79 Sparviero and six SM.84 torpedo-bombers)
102° Gruppo (36 Ju 87 Stuka dive-bombers)
25° Gruppo/155° Gruppo (27 MC.202 Folgore fighters)
46° Gruppo/47° Gruppo (20 CR.42 Falco fighters)
Special Force (one SM.79 Sparviero, one CANT Z.1007b Alcione, two RE.2001 Falco 2s)

Fliegerkorps II (Luftwaffe)
Sicily:
1./Aufklärungs GR (F).122 (seven Ju 88 long-range reconnaissance aircraft), Catania and Elmas
2./Aufklärungs GR (F).122 (seven Ju 88 long-range reconnaissance aircraft), Trapani
Kampfgeschwader 606 (22 Ju 88 medium bombers), Catania
Kampfgeschwader 806 (21 Ju 88 medium bombers), Catania
II./Kampfgeschwader 77 (16 Ju 88 medium bombers), Comiso and Gerbini
III./Kampfgeschwader 77 (15 Ju 88 medium bombers), Comiso and Gerbini
Lehrgeschwader 1 (28 Ju 88 medium bombers), Gerbini
I./Sturzkampfgeschwader 3 (26 Ju 87D dive-bombers), Trapani
II./Kampfgeschwader 26 (six He 111 torpedo-bombers), Gerbini
I./Kampfgeschwader 54 (20 Ju 88 torpedo-bombers)
I./Nachtjagdgeschwader 2 (12 Bf 110 night-fighters), Catania
II./Jagdgeschwader 53 (18 Bf 109G fighters), Gerbini and Comiso
Sardinia:
I./Jagdgeschwader 77 (13 Bf 109G fighters), Elmas
Pantelleria:
Det., Kampfgeschwader 53 (three Bf 109G fighters)
Det., Kampfgeschwader 54 (eight Ju 88 torpedo-bombers)

OPPOSING PLANS

ALLIES

The decision to send a relief convoy to Malta was taken by the British Chiefs of Staff on 15 June. Vice Admiral Syfret would lead the operation. He received his orders in the Admiralty on 14 July. Waiting for him there were his senior commanders, Rear Admiral Burrough and Rear Admiral Lyster. For the next month these three officers set about planning this complex operation.

Pedestal had to take place before Malta's supplies ran out on 7 September. The span of 10–16 August was duly selected due to the lack of moonlight during the last days of the operation. That gave the planning team a month to assemble the ships. Ironically, what really helped them was the biggest disaster to befall an Allied convoy during the war. On 27 June convoy PQ-17 sailed from Iceland, bound for Archangel. Its 35 merchantmen were protected by a close escort. The air and U-boat attacks began on 2 July, but two days later the Admiralty learned that the German battleship *Tirpitz* intended to fall upon the convoy. So, First Sea Lord Admiral Sir Dudley Pound ordered the escort to withdraw and the convoy to scatter. This proved disastrous. Although *Tirpitz* never sailed, 24 merchant ships were sunk by aircraft and U-boats. After this debacle further Arctic convoys were suspended until the coming of winter. For Syfret, though, this helped his own operation. Now, warships from the Home Fleet would be available to take part in the *Pedestal* operation.

The first task was to assemble a convoy. Fourteen fast merchant ships were gathered in British ports, including one fast tanker, the *Ohio*. These all had extra AA guns fitted, manned by naval crews. As a deception, the convoy was given the designation WS.5.21S, a prefix that usually indicated a 'Winston Special'

Rear Admiral Lyster, pictured on the right, on board the carrier *Illustrious* in late 1940. Lyster had planned the Taranto raid of November 1940, and by mid-1942 was the Royal Navy's most experienced carrier strike force commander. Pictured beside him is Commander James Robertson, who was in charge of flying operations on board *Illustrious*.

convoy, bound from home waters to the Suez Canal, by way of the Cape of Good Hope.

Essentially, this would be a repeat of Operation *Harpoon*. A close escort (Force X) would accompany the convoy through to Malta. The covering force (Force Z) would only accompany it as far as the Narrows. Then, to avoid significant losses, it would break off and return to Gibraltar. Syfret insisted on providing the convoy with air cover from fleet carriers. These were vital assets, and so they had to be well-protected by AA cruisers and destroyers. In *Harpoon* the close escort had been too weak; only the reluctance of the Italians to press home their attack saved the convoy from being overwhelmed. This time, Burrough, who would command Force X, made sure it was more powerful than before, and included minesweepers to cut a path for the convoy through the Axis minefields.

The First Sea Lord Sir Dudley Pound was the man who authorized the creation of the *Pedestal* convoy, although this decision was then ratified at a meeting of the British Chiefs of Staff in mid-June 1942. His planning staff were then temporarily seconded to Vice Admiral Syfret, to give him the staff capability to organize *Pedestal* at short notice.

Other elements were then added. One of these was a 'Club Run', the flying-off of RAF Spitfires from a carrier, to reinforce Malta's air defences. This was codenamed Operation *Bellows*, and would take place concurrently with *Pedestal*. The fleet carrier *Furious* was earmarked for this, and would accompany the convoy until she reached her launch position on 11 August. She and her escort would then return to Gibraltar. Lyster was well aware that the successful repulse of Axis air attacks relied on good fighter direction. So, Operation *Berserk* was added, using aircraft from the old carrier *Argus* to stand in for the enemy. She would accompany Lyster's carriers during the run south to Gibraltar. *Argus* would then assist with the fighter-control training of *Pedestal*'s aircraft and fighter-control assets. Then, on reaching Gibraltar she would part company, after transferring her six Sea Hurricanes to *Victorious*.

Four other minor strands were also included in *Pedestal*. First, two replenishment groups (forces R and W) were earmarked to refuel the escorts as they sailed south to Gibraltar, and then passed through the Western Mediterranean. They would then return to Gibraltar. Two tugs accompanying Force R would then be transferred to Force X, and would accompany the convoy to Malta. The Admiralty used Operation *Pedestal* to solve another problem. Since Operation *Harpoon*, the two merchant ships which had reached Malta were still there. So, in a mission codenamed Operation *Ascendant*, these would attempt to make it through to Gibraltar, escorted by a destroyer and an escort destroyer. This would be timed to coincide with the transit of the Operation *Pedestal* convoy through the Narrows.

Finally, it was hoped that Admiral Harwood would be able to stage a diversion to the east of Malta. This, designated Operation *MG.3*, would be a repeat of the decoy mission that had formed part of Operation *Vigorous*. A well-defended convoy of four merchant ships would approach Malta from

The problem of replenishing the British escorts during *Pedestal* presented a challenge to the operation's planners. Refuelling at sea was in its infancy. Here, an escort destroyer breaks away from an aircraft carrier, after taking on fuel from her in 1942.

the east as the *Pedestal* convoy reached the Narrows. The decoy convoy would then return to port under cover of darkness. Harwood also approved another diversion, Operation *MG.4*, which involved the night bombardment of Rhodes by British light cruisers.

The planning of Operation *Pedestal* was a major administrative task, and involved the routing of warships from as far away as the Indian Ocean and the South Atlantic. It is a testimony to the skills of the Admiralty planners, and Vice Admiral Syfret's team, that this was accomplished in the short time available. Finally, on 27 July, everything was ready. That day, the battleship *Nelson* arrived in Scapa Flow, after being sent there from Freetown in West Africa. Syfret then hoisted his flag in her, and embarked his staff. Two days later, on 29 July, he hosted a meeting on board her for his senior officers. Here, the detailed orders for Operation *Pedestal* were issued. Two days later, the flagship slipped out of Scapa Flow, and shaped a course for Gibraltar, effectively marking the start of Operation *Pedestal*.

AXIS

The Axis fully expected the Allies would attempt to relieve Malta, and so had developed plans to counter this. What limited their effectiveness was a lack of cooperation. While Feldmarschall Kesselring commanded all German forces in the theatre, he had no similar control over Italian forces. Instead, any plans had to be developed in cooperation with the Italian Commando

Axis defences in the Western Mediterranean, August 1942

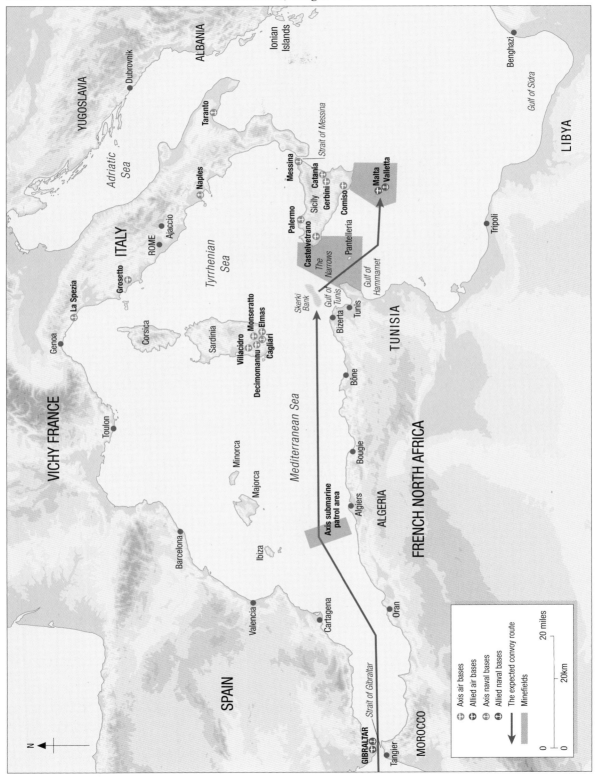

YUGOSLAVIA

ALBANIA

Ionian
Islands

Dubrovnik

*Adriatic
Sea*

Taranto

Benghazi

Gulf of Sidra

Strait of Messina

Messina

Naples

Sicily Catania

Gerbini

Comiso

Malta
Valletta

Palermo

ROME

ITALY

Ajaccio

*Tyrrhenian
Sea*

Castelvetrano

*The
Narrows*

Pantelleria

*Gulf of
Hammamet*

Grosetto

LIBYA

Tripoli

La Spezia

Corsica

Villacidro
Monseratto

Decimomannu   Elmas

Cagliari

*Skerki
Bank*

*Gulf of
Tunis*

Bizerta

Tunis

Genoa

Sardinia

TUNISIA

VICHY FRANCE

Toulon

Bône

Minorca

Mediterranean Sea

Bougie

FRENCH NORTH AFRICA

Majorca

Axis submarine
patrol area

Barcelona

Ibiza

Algiers

ALGERIA

Valencia

Cartagena

Oran

MOROCCO

SPAIN

Strait of Gibraltar

GIBRALTAR

Tangier

N

Axis air bases
Allied air bases
Axis naval bases
Allied naval bases
The expected convoy route
Minefields

20 miles

20km

0

0

29

An Italian SM.79 torpedo-bomber, flying over a British escort after dropping her torpedo. These bombers were robust, and if well handled, they proved excellent anti-shipping aircraft. Attacks were usually carried out at altitudes of less than 50m. The Italian 45cm (17.7in.) torpedo had a range of 3,300m, running at 40 knots.

Supremo (High Command), while naval matters had to be agreed with the Italian Supermarina (Naval Headquarters). Even the Kriegsmarine in the Mediterranean was semi-autonomous, despite Kesselring's nominal control of it, and operational details needed to be agreed with Konteradmiral Eberhard Weichold, the Kriegsmarine's liaison officer attached to the Supermarina in Rome. This said, as head of Luftflotte II, Kesselring enjoyed a reasonably amicable relationship with his Italian counterpart, Generale Fougier, the Chief of Staff of the Regia Aeronautica.

The Supermarina envisaged three likely Allied moves. The first was a convoy escorted through the Narrows, supported by battleships and aircraft carriers. A variant was the same, only the British capital ships would turn back before reaching the Narrows. The Supermarina also considered the enemy might invade Sardinia, placing the Allies within bomber range of the Italian mainland. The fourth option was a major British naval sortie into the Tyrrhenian Sea, in an attempt to force the Italian battle fleet to sea, which would allow the British to bring it to battle. The two Malta convoy options were the most likely, though, and of these, it was thought unlikely the British would risk their capital ships in the waters south of Sicily. In any case, a major sortie by the Italian battle fleet would have drained the Italian navy's fuel reserves, which had been in short supply. So, instead of countering a Malta convoy with the battle fleet, the Supermarina deployed da Zara's two cruiser divisions, a force considered powerful enough to deal with the British convoy's close escort, as long as it wasn't reinforced by capital ships.

The Italians developed a staged series of defensive measures. The first was a screen of German U-boats, Italian submarines and Axis reconnaissance aircraft, which would detect any approaching enemy force and shadow it. If possible, the submarine patrol line would be able to whittle down the enemy's strength before it reached the Narrows. A group of submarines

A German Ju 88 bomber, armed with four SC 250 bombs. These 250kg high-explosive bombs, carried by both Ju 88s and Ju 87s, could be fused to detonate on impact, or else detonated after a delay of up to 17 seconds. They also had a limited armour-piercing capability, as evidenced by the ease with which they pierced the 3in. armoured deck of *Indomitable*.

would then deploy around the Skerki Channel, to fall upon the convoy as it passed. In the Narrows itself, and around Malta, dense minefields had been sown. These would constrict and slow the convoy, making it an easier target for Axis bombers.

The lack of cooperation between the Regia Aeronautica and Fliegerkorps II meant that fully coordinated attacks were impossible. However, shared intelligence meant that both air forces would know where the enemy was, and so would be able to launch their own attacks on the convoy. Meanwhile, if any attempt was made to approach Malta from the east, Fliegerkorps X stationed in Greece and Crete would be able to intercept the enemy convoy. Like the Western Mediterranean, submarine patrol lines were established in the Eastern Mediterranean, supported by regular reconnaissance flights.

Finally, although both the Regia Aeronautica and Fliegerkorps II were heavily committed supporting Rommel's Axis army in Egypt, air formations were moved from North Africa to Sicily. The Fliegerkorps had lost most of its specialist torpedo-bomber units, which had been reassigned to Norway that summer. However, 28 Ju 88s from I. and II./LG 1 belonging to Fliegerkorps X were transferred from Crete to Sicily on 11–12 August. At the same time, the Ju 88s of KG 606 and KG 806 were transferred from southern France to Sicily, to further boost the Luftwaffe's strength. Fortunately for Kesselring, the Italians already had over 60 torpedo-bombers in Sicily and Sardinia. Like the Germans, the Italians also redeployed units on the eve of the campaign. These included 32° Stormo, which were moved from Apulia to Sardinia, 105° Stormo which arrived from Tuscany, and 2° and 153° Gruppi moved from Rome and Turin respectively. Fougier also redeployed his units within the theatre itself, sending 102° and 132° Stormi to airfields closer to the Narrows. Finally, once it was confirmed another convoy was gathering at Gibraltar, both Fougier and Kesselring stepped up their long-range reconnaissance flights over the Western Mediterranean.

OPERATION *PEDESTAL*

Operation *Pedestal* marked the largest concentration of British naval power so far in the war. It was a testimony to its planning that the assembly of this armada went so smoothly. The exception to this was its secrecy. Blunders were made, which were later catalogued in a Ministry of War Transport enquiry. When the ships were being loaded, packing crates were labelled 'Malta', a gift to any spy, while in the various assembly ports the convoy's destination was widely known. Even the Convoy Commodore was told by stevedores he was sailing to Malta. It amounted to a major breach of security. This in turn made Operation *Pedestal* all the more dangerous. Regardless, in late July, as the merchantmen were loaded with their cargoes, the final preparations were made for what would be the most important convoy operation of the war.

THE FIRST LEG

The key element of this whole enterprise was the convoy itself. Its ships were loaded in Bristol, Liverpool and Glasgow, then assembled off Gourock in the Clyde. The various types of cargo were spread equally among the ships. For example, the cargo ship *Empire Hope* carried ammunition, fuel stowed in jerrycans and tanker bowsers, medical equipment, military stores, food, coal and luxuries such as alcohol, cigarettes and chocolate. The exception was the tanker *Ohio*, but to reduce risk, she carried her cargo in large oil drums. Convoy WS.5.21S was scheduled to depart from the Clyde on 1 August.

In fact, the assembly was only completed on Sunday 2 August. At noon, a convoy conference was held on board Rear Admiral Burrough's flagship *Nigeria*, attended by all merchant ship captains and the senior captains of the close escort. The briefing concentrated on the importance of station-keeping, of speed, and the impossibility of the merchantmen stopping to pick up casualties. That would be the job of the escorts. Above all, it emphasized that this convoy was of vital importance to the survival of Malta. It was only when the captains returned to their ships that their crews were told of their destination. Then, at 1800hrs that evening, the Convoy Commodore's ship SS *Port Chalmers* got under way. Behind her, in line astern, the other 12 merchant ships and the tanker did the same. The voyage of Convoy WS.5.21S had begun. The *Nigeria* followed astern. Other warships joined them as they steamed south.

Rear Admiral Burrough, commander of Force X, the *Pedestal* convoy's close escort, is pictured here shaking hands with Captain Mason of the SS *Ohio*, after a pre-convoy briefing in the Clyde on board Burrough's flagship *Nigeria*.

The following morning, the convoy was formed up into two parallel columns, making 14 knots. Then, for the rest of the day, station-keeping and convoy formation exercises were practised, until Burrough was happy the merchant skippers knew what was expected of them. Meanwhile, other ships from Force X and Force Z were at sea, and would rendezvous with the convoy during the coming days. These included aircraft carriers under the operational control of Rear Admiral Lyster, flying his flag in *Victorious*. One of these was the small carrier *Argus*, included solely for Operation *Berserk*, an exercise designed to test ship-based fighter control among the force's carriers and escorts.

The carrier *Indomitable* was steaming north from Freetown in West Africa, accompanied by the AA cruiser *Phoebe*. So, too, was Force W, the fleet oiler *Abbeydale*. Another carrier, *Eagle*, was about to leave Gibraltar to join them in the Atlantic, accompanied by the AA cruiser *Charybdis*. A fourth carrier, *Furious*, was included to make a 'Club Run', and had been expected to join the convoy in the Clyde. She, though, had hit a snag. On 30 July she embarked 41 Spitfire Mark Vs, but it was discovered their new oversized propellers made it impossible to fly off the carrier due to the hump in her flight deck. She had to wait for replacement propellers, which arrived early on 4 August. Captain Tom Bulteel then put to sea, as his crew worked through the night to modify the aircraft. A Spitfire was successfully flown off the following morning. Bulteel then set off at full speed to rendezvous with Lyster.

On the morning of 3 August, as the convoy steamed through the Western Approaches, Vice Admiral Syfret's flagship *Nelson* and her sister ship *Rodney* joined them. All that day and the next, the convoy exercises continued as it ran south through rough seas and grey skies under Syfret's experienced eye. After passing west of Cape Finisterre early on 5 August, the convoy headed almost due south, albeit zigzagging as it went. Progress was good, so

For Operation *Pedestal* the Admiralty gathered together a powerful force of warships, including three fleet carriers. Here, *Indomitable* and *Eagle* are following in line astern behind *Victorious* during the voyage south to the Mediterranean.

Syfret reduced the convoy's speed to 12 knots. Meanwhile far to the south, 300 miles west of Gibraltar, Lyster's carriers commenced Operation *Berserk*. Lyster also practised the defensive scheme his aircraft would adopt in the Mediterranean. Here, the Fulmars of *Victorious* would provide low-level cover against torpedo-bombers, while the Martlets and Sea Hurricanes of the other carriers would create a high-altitude screen against enemy dive-bombers. After completing the exercise, the carriers steamed north to join the convoy.

Lyster rendezvoused with the convoy the following morning, 300 miles off the Portuguese coast. Their job done, *Argus* and her escorts went on to Gibraltar. That day, Lyster's carriers tried to refuel from *Abbeydale*, but the oiler's crew were unable to maintain a connection. This was a problem, as Syfret had planned to refuel all of Force Z, to avoid having to put into Gibraltar. Fortunately, Syfret was having more luck replenishing from RFA *Brown Ranger*, which had now joined them. Most of the escorts were topped up, but it was now clear that refuelling at Gibraltar was a necessity. So, Syfret organized this as the convoy steamed south. By the evening of 8 August, they had taken up a circular holding position 40 miles west of Gibraltar. That night, led by *Indomitable*, warships put in to refuel, while others replenished from *Brown Ranger* and the hired tanker *San Claudio*.

The following day passed uneventfully, as the refuelling continued. Spanish fishing boats had been spotted, though, and an Italian radio broadcast told of their arrival off Gibraltar. This meant the enemy knew they were coming. Finally, at 2000hrs that evening, the convoy got under way again, and passed through the Strait of Gibraltar in two columns. By 2300hrs, after Cape Spartel in Morocco was sighted, a fog descended. Still, by 0230hrs on Monday 10 August, they had passed Gibraltar. The convoy had now entered the Mediterranean.

THROUGH THE WESTERN MEDITERRANEAN, 10–11 AUGUST

The convoy was still not fully formed up. Several warships were still refuelling at Gibraltar, and joined the others as the day wore on. The smaller escorts still needed topping up, though, so late on 9 August Force R steamed on ahead, to replenish them when the convoy caught up. To reduce the risk from enemy submarines, seven destroyers were sent ahead to protect the oilers. At dawn on 10 August, Captain Richard Onslow's destroyers reached Force R, 250 miles east of Gibraltar, and screened the oilers, while taking turns to refuel. As the convoy approached, several cruisers and destroyers forged ahead to refuel, too. When the convoy passed to the south, the AA cruiser *Cairo* was detached to protect the oilers, before rejoining Force X later that evening, together with Onslow's destroyers.

Meanwhile, reports of the convoy's approach had reached Kesselring, and so reconnaissance flights were stepped up, and vessels and aircraft squadrons were placed on alert. This included the submarines which were even now heading west to form their patrol line north of Algiers, astride the convoy's path. The only Axis resource which didn't react was the Italian battle fleet, which remained in port due to a chronic shortage of fuel. The patrol line's submarines reached their station that evening. Then, at 0150hrs on Tuesday 11 August, at the northern end of the patrol line the Italian submarine *Uarsciek* detected the sound of propellers. Tenente di Vascello Targia headed west to investigate, and shortly after 0300hrs he spotted Force R, the tankers screened by four corvettes. Targia reported the sighting, and at 0340hrs he fired three torpedoes. They missed, but when one porpoised to the surface, it was spotted by the corvette *Coltsfoot*. This was the opening shot of the *Pedestal* battle.

This photograph captures something of the power of the force assembled for Operation *Pedestal*. Shown here is the British fleet carrier *Eagle*, with *Victorious* and *Indomitable* off her starboard quarter, on 11 August after entering the Mediterranean.

Depth charges detonating astern of a British destroyer. Detecting a submarine in the Western Mediterranean was problematic due to thermal layers there, but once a boat was detected, multiple patterns of depth charges could be dropped speedily from the escort, set to explode at the probable depth of the contact.

By noon on 11 August the *Pedestal* convoy was directly north of Algiers, zigzagging along a base course to the west, making 13 knots. Earlier that morning the convoy had been sighted by both Italian and German reconnaissance aircraft. Among the Italian submarines in the patrol line were two German U-boats, *U-73* and *U-205*. Kapitänleutnant Franz-Georg Reschke of *U-205* spotted the convoy, but was unable to close with it, being forced to remain submerged because of the British aircraft flying overhead. Kapitänleutnant Helmut Rosenbaum of *U-73*, though, was in a much better position. At 1100hrs he sighted masts through the periscope, and then spotted a large vessel, escorted by destroyers some 8,000m distant. However, she steamed away to the north-east and disappeared from sight. She was *Furious*, breaking off from the convoy to conduct Operation *Bellows* – her 'Club Run' delivery of Spitfires to Malta.

Then, at 1226hrs, Rosenbaum spotted numerous masts through his periscope. A little later, destroyers passed overhead without detecting him. Rosenbaum knew that local conditions were ideal for submarines. Temperature differences between layers of cold water from the Atlantic passing over warmer Mediterranean water created thermoclines. These transition layers were hard for sonar pulses to penetrate. So, while he stayed below the thermocline, he was relatively safe from detection. Ten minutes later he raised his periscope again, and spotted the convoy to the north-west, steaming east. Rosenbaum turned north and crept forward to intercept. Fourteen minutes later he spotted the carrier *Eagle*, the last ship on the starboard side of the convoy. So, Rosenbaum dropped down again below the thermocline, and continued his approach. In between him and his quarry was a line of six destroyers, all sending out sonar pulses.

U-73 crept under them, undetected below the thermocline, and at 1302hrs Rosenbaum raised his attack periscope. He spotted a Dido-class AA cruiser, followed by *Eagle*, with another destroyer astern. Beyond these were at least eight merchant ships. It was a U-boat commander's dream. At 1315hrs, *Eagle* was just 800m away, having just turned to port to launch aircraft. Rosenbaum fired a spread of four torpedoes, set at a depth of 6m. He then turned away and dived, to reduce the impact of the inevitable depth-charging. After 30 seconds they heard four loud explosions, meaning all their torpedoes had hit the carrier.

The torpedoes had been perfectly spaced, striking *Eagle* at 40ft intervals along her port beam, 18ft below the waterline. Two had struck her machinery spaces, and as the sea flooded into her port engine and boiler rooms, the carrier listed rapidly to port. Shortly after the last hit, her flight deck was

The aircraft carrier *Eagle* (right) rolls over to port after being hit by four torpedoes fired from *U-73* in the Western Mediterranean on 12 August. The convoy and its escorts had been lucky: there were several Axis submarines and U-boats in the area at the time, but the elderly carrier was their only victim.

canted over at a 30-degree angle. The Sea Hurricanes ranged on her flight deck slipped into the sea, and the way came off the ship as she lost power. Hundreds of men jumped clear as she began capsizing, but many more were still trapped below decks as the carrier rolled over. *Eagle* sank in just eight minutes. As they crept away, the crew of *U-73* heard a succession of underwater explosions.

Two miles away on *Nelson*, Syfret ordered the convoy to make an immediate hard turn to port, followed by another to starboard, until he realized where the attack had come from. Then, at 1319hrs the convoy turned away to the south. Meanwhile, the tug *Jaunty* and the destroyers *Lookout* and *Laforey* began pulling survivors from the water, while Commander John Broome in *Keppel* led six destroyers in a depth-charging frenzy, the concussions felt painfully by the survivors in the water. In all, 972 men were rescued, including Captain Lachlan Mackintosh. Another 233 were lost with their ship. Syfret ordered the destroyers to transfer their survivors to *Furious*'s escorts *Keppel* and *Venomous*, which were about to return to Gibraltar. *Jaunty*, with *Amazon* as escort, was sent to join Force R to the west, and would return to Gibraltar with them. In hindsight that was

The survivors of the aircraft carrier *Eagle*, pictured coming aboard the destroyer *Lookout* in the early afternoon of 12 August. The destroyer's boats, and ones from *Laforey* and the tug *Jaunty*, were used in the rescue. In all, 927 of *Eagle*'s crew were recovered from the water.

The *Pedestal* convoy's progress, 11–12 August 1942

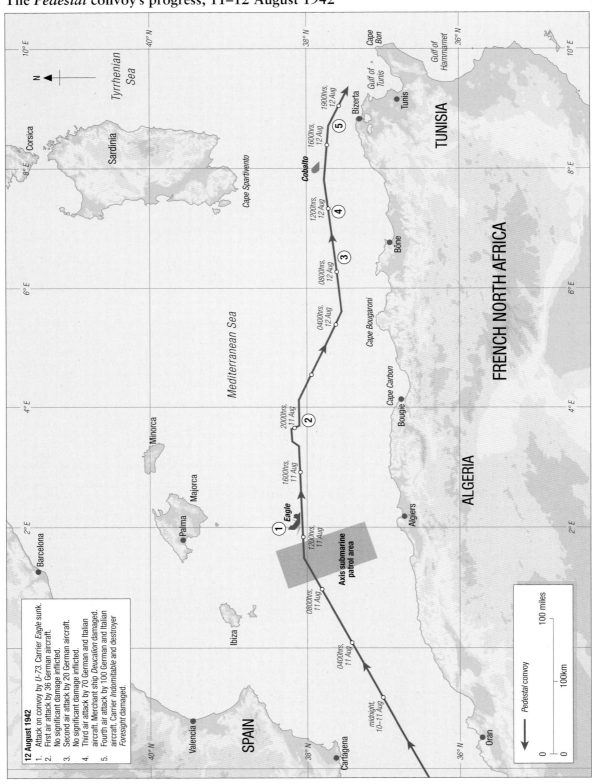

12 August 1942

1. Attack on convoy by *U-73*. Carrier *Eagle* sunk.
2. First air attack by 36 German aircraft. No significant damage inflicted.
3. Second air attack by 20 German aircraft. No significant damage inflicted.
4. Third air attack by 70 German and Italian aircraft. Merchant ship *Deucalion* damaged.
5. Fourth air attack by 100 German and Italian aircraft. Carrier *Indomitable* and destroyer *Foresight* damaged.

Pedestal convoy

100 miles

100km

a mistake, as the rescue tug would have been invaluable if she had remained with Force X.

Meanwhile, Operation *Bellows* was completed according to plan. At 1218hrs *Furious* left the convoy and moved to her launching-off position, eight miles to the north. The Spitfires began flying off at 1230hrs, and although the operation was halted after *Eagle* was hit, it was resumed at 1350hrs, and completed an hour later. In all, 38 Spitfires fitted with drop tanks were launched, and began their 565-mile flight to Malta's Hal-Far airfield. Two destroyers protected the carrier during *Bellows*, while the others hunted for *U-73*. The 'Club Run' complete, *Furious* and her two escorts turned west towards Gibraltar, and at 1800hrs they were joined by Broome and his destroyers, after a fruitless hunt. The voyage west was uneventful until 0014hrs, when the destroyer *Wolverine* detected a radar contact ahead. Lieutenant-Commander Peter Gretton steamed to intercept it, and encountered the Italian submarine *Dagabur* on the surface. *Wolverine* rammed her squarely amidships, cutting *Dagabur* in half. She sank with all hands. The damaged destroyer eventually reached Gibraltar safely, a day behind *Furious* and her other escorts.

Meanwhile, the *Pedestal* convoy continued on its zigzagging course towards the east, shadowed all the while by enemy reconnaissance planes. At 1900hrs, when submarines were sighted to the south, Syfret diverted the convoy to the north of its original track, to avoid them. Then, at 2030hrs, aircraft were spotted on radar, approaching from the east. Fighters were scrambled, and at 2056hrs five Ju 88s were sighted, flying in an arrowhead at 8,000ft. An AA barrage was put up, but only one of the bombers was hit. The others dropped their bombs around *Victorious*, but none of them struck her. Then, six He 111s and 20 Ju 88s from KG 26 and KG 54 appeared, and this time the barrage claimed two bombers. The remainder released their torpedoes at long range and turned away, but scored no hits. The *Pedestal* convoy had just survived its first air attack.

However, as the fighters returned to their carriers, they found themselves being shot at by their own ships. Some of the Sea Hurricanes were now all but out of fuel. After delaying flying through their own fleet's barrage, some even crash-landed on *Victorious* as their fuel ran out. Seeing the problem, and disregarding the high threat of a submarine attack, Captain Thomas Troubridge of *Indomitable* switched on his deck landing lights, along with just about every other light in the carrier. So, as darkness fell, the last of the fighters were able to land safely. The coming of night meant a respite from air attacks. While the sonar operators maintained their vigil, the air crews and AA gunners grabbed what sleep they could. By midnight the convoy was around 160 miles from the spot where *Eagle* had been sunk. Some 50 miles to the west 12 Ju 88s from III./KG 717 attacked Force R without success. Late the following day, Force R reached Gibraltar safely.

THE SECONDARY OPERATIONS, 10–12 AUGUST

Late on 10 August, while the *Pedestal* convoy was passing Gibraltar, another convoy was preparing to leave Malta. The merchant ships *Orari* and *Troilus* had reached Malta in June during Operation *Harpoon*. Now, in Operation *Ascendant*, they were to return to Gibraltar, accompanied by the destroyer

Matchless and the escort destroyer *Badsworth*. Captain J. Pilditch of *Troilus*, the convoy commodore for *Harpoon*, also commanded *Ascendant*. Although their evening departure was secret, word had spread, and the Maltese lined the harbour front to wave them off. They headed south-west at 13 knots, until they were clear of the minefields around Malta. Near the island of Lampedusa they turned north, heading towards Cape Bon, the north-eastern tip of Tunisia. That night they painted red and white Italian air recognition markings on their foredecks. At dawn they reduced speed to 8 knots and formed into line ahead, with *Matchless* leading. The aim was to look like an Italian convoy.

Late on 11 August they reached Cape Bon, but at 2130hrs Lieutenant-Commander John Mowlam, of *Matchless* spotted a warship ahead. It was the Italian destroyer *Lanzerotto Malocello*, laying mines close inshore. Mowlam turned *Matchless* to starboard and opened fire. The Italian destroyer fired back, before the protagonists were lost in the darkness. The rest of the night passed without incident, and before dawn they removed their Italian air recognition markings, as they would soon come within range of Gibraltar-based aircraft. Dawn on 12 August found them north of the Tunisian-Algerian border. It was a dangerous time as the *Pedestal* convoy was just over the horizon to the north. During the day several Axis aircraft 'buzzed' them, but it was mid-afternoon, while approaching Bougie, that a Ju 88 dropped down for a closer look. The British escorts opened fire, and the bomber was hit. She flew off inshore, trailing smoke. After that there were no further brushes with the enemy. The following day their air escort arrived, and the small *Ascendant* convoy entered Gibraltar at 1100hrs on 14 August.

As the *Ascendant* convoy was leaving Malta, another convoy sailed from Port Said, Egypt. This was the decoy convoy MG.3, made up of three merchantmen, escorted by three light cruisers and ten destroyers. Early the following morning, Rear Admiral Vian in *Cleopatra* sailed from Haifa, accompanied by another cruiser, a merchantman and five destroyers. The two groups rendezvoused, and then steamed west throughout 11 August. Inevitably, they were spotted by Luftwaffe reconnaissance planes operating from Crete. Then, after dark, Vian led part of his force off to bombard the airfields on Rhodes. The convoy, then split into three groups, and returned to Haifa, Port Said and Beirut.

Throughout the next day fake radio messages were transmitted to suggest MG.3 was still heading towards Malta, and aircraft operating from Egypt dropped flares over its supposed position, to simulate convoy activity. Surprisingly, the Axis never reacted to this deception. The Rhodes bombardment was carried out successfully on the evening of 12 August, and Vian then withdrew. Apart from being shadowed by reconnaissance aircraft, they saw no sign of the enemy, and the Italian battle fleet never put to sea. The irony of all this was that the four merchant ships could probably have made it through to Malta without incident, if the MG.3 operation had involved a real convoy rather than a dummy one.

THE WESTERN MEDITERRANEAN, 12 AUGUST

On Wednesday 12 August, sunrise came at 0630hrs, as did the convoy's aerial stalkers. Throughout the day reconnaissance aircraft shadowed the convoy, but for the most part the British carrier-borne fighters left them alone. At dawn the convoy was heading east at 16 knots, 30 miles north of the Algerian coast. Intelligence reports suggested that 50 miles ahead lay another line of Axis submarines to the north of the Galite Islands. In fact, some of the submarines were much closer. At 0741hrs three torpedo tracks were spotted off the starboard bow of *Kenya*, but Captain Alfred Russell successfully threaded the tracks. The assailant was hunted by several destroyers, but managed to evade

The battleship *Rodney*, photographed by an Italian reconnaissance plane during 12 August. Essentially, she and her sister *Nelson*, flagship of Vice Admiral Syfret, were included in the escort to counter the Italian battle fleet if it made a sortie.

them. The first air attack came a little after 0900hrs. A force of approaching bombers was detected to the east, and the patrolling British fighters were sent to intercept them. In the dogfight that followed, three Ju 88 bombers from LG 1 were shot down, and several others jettisoned their bombs and withdrew. Six others released their bombs over the fleet, but scored no hits. Two of these attackers were shot down, as was a Sea Hurricane from *Victorious*.

Then, at 0935hrs the destroyer *Fury* reported a sonar contact to the south. She and *Foresight* left to investigate, but the contact eluded them, and at 1000hrs the hunt was called off. The contact was Tenente Andreotti's boat *Brin*, which at the time had been shadowing the convoy from its starboard beam. Two other boats from the first patrol line, *Uarsciek* and *U-73*, were following it from astern. At 1140hrs, when *Pathfinder* detected a contact to the north, she and *Zetland* dropped depth charges, but contact

A large-scale attack on the convoy by the Regia Aeronautica. By mid-1942 the majority of these SM.79 Sparviero (Sparrowhawk) bombers had been adapted to carry torpedoes. This grainy photograph was taken from one of their companions during the attack in the early afternoon of 12 August.

was lost. The contact was *U-205*, which had been approaching the convoy from the north-west. By noon the *Pedestal* convoy was passing to the north of the Algerian-Tunisian border. Then, radar picked up 85 enemy aircraft approaching from the east.

These were Italian planes, flying from airfields in Sardinia. The attacks came in a series of waves, which gave the British fighters a greater chance of disrupting the attacking formations. Ten of these were SM.84s from the 32° Stormo, armed with the Motobomba. These were 360kg aerial mines, which were dropped by parachute in the path of their target. When the Motobomba hit the water, the parachute was released. A gyroscope set it on its course, at a depth of 3m. Compressed air was used as a propellant, which left no wake. The mine then circled around in a steadily enlarging spiral until it either struck a target or ran out of propellant, at which point it self-destructed. Each bomber carried two of these secret weapons. However, in their debut operational performance the bomber crews were surprised by the British fighters, and so they all dropped their mines prematurely. At 1215hrs Syfret turned the convoy away to the north and the Motobombas were deftly avoided. Ten minutes later the convoy resumed its original course.

The main assault involved SM.79 and SM.84 torpedo-bombers escorted by Falco 2 fighters. The British fighters drove off the 10 SM.84s of the 32° Stormo, but the wave of 21 SM.79s remained intact. In all, 21 torpedo-bombers attacked the convoy from port, and nine more from starboard, each prong covered by fighters. The warships threw up an AA barrage, and this led many of the Italians to release their torpedoes early. Others pressed on, though, despite two bombers and a fighter being shot down. The rest then dropped their torpedoes. Their targets were the British capital ships. *Nelson* and *Rodney* used their 16in. guns to throw up a 'splash barrage', seeking to prematurely detonate the torpedoes. While this was taking place, by way of a diversion, eight bomb-armed CR.42s attacked the escorting destroyers. All of the bombs and torpedoes missed, but the assault helped screen the approach of two further groups of Axis aircraft.

The first was an Italian Sezione Speciale (Special Section) approaching from the north, made up of a CANT Z.1007bis, an SM.79 and four Re.2001 or G.50 fighters. The SM.79 carried a 1,000kg bomb, fitted with a radio-controlled guidance system. After pointing the bomber at *Indomitable*, the pilot bailed out. The bomber was then guided to its target from the accompanying CANT. However, the radio guidance failed, and the bomber flew on to crash in the Algerian mountains. Accompanying the Sezione

Speciale were a pair of Re.2001 Falco 2s armed with two 50kg fragmentation bombs apiece. At 1345hrs they attacked *Victorious*, whose gunners mistook them for Hurricanes about to land. Two bombs hit the flight deck, but didn't cause any significant damage.

Next it was the turn of the Luftwaffe. At 1238hrs a wave of 37 Ju 88s escorted by Me 109 fighters drew near the convoy, with small groups approaching from different directions. British fighters tried to disrupt the attackers before they reached the AA barrage thrown up by the escorts. A dozen bombers in all successfully penetrated the barrage and at 1300hrs they dropped their bombs over the convoy. All but three missed. A stick of bombs hit the *Deucalion*, though, the leading ship in the convoy's port column, buckling her hull plates and causing heavy flooding. Captain Ramsay Brown stopped the ship to deal with any flooding, and while the escort destroyer *Bramham* stood by her, the rest of the convoy steamed on. By then the German bombers had flown off, pursued by British fighters. At that point some of *Deucalion*'s crew took to the boats and rowed off, only to be rounded up and returned to their ship by Lieutenant Edward Baines of *Bramham*.

An hour after the attack, *Deucalion* was able to get under way again, making 10 knots. So, with *Bramham* beside her, *Deucalion* limped off towards the Tunisian coast. Captain Brown still hoped to reach Malta. The Axis attacks, though, were far from over. A little over an hour after the air attack, the convoy reached the patrol line of enemy submarines deployed to the north of the Galite Islands. At 1410hrs lookouts on the destroyer *Tartar* spotted a submarine on the surface, between the convoy and the coast. It was the Italian submarine *Granito*. She was depth-charged, and although the boat survived, by being forced to submerge it missed its chance to intercept the convoy. After that, Syfret had the escorts drop depth charges occasionally, to deter any attempt to sneak past them.

Then, at 1640hrs, another torpedo was spotted by *Tartar*. Commander John Tyrwhitt steamed towards an Asdic contact, accompanied by *Lookout*. The torpedo was one of four fired by the Italian submarine *Ebro*. All of them missed their target. Tenente Franco's boat was depth-charged, but managed to sneak away, as did the *Avorio* operating nearby. Meanwhile, on the north side of the convoy *Pathfinder* and *Zetland* detected a contact, and again they dropped depth charges, seemingly without effect. In fact, these damaged the Italian submarine *Cobalto*. Her buoyancy tanks had been ruptured, and at 1645hrs she broke the surface two miles behind the convoy.

This extremely grainy photograph is the best surviving record of a very dramatic moment: the ramming of the Italian submarine *Cobalto* by the destroyer *Ithuriel* on 12 August. This was a largely unnecessary act of bravado, as the submarine was already damaged and had been forced to the surface. Later, Vice Admiral Syfret was unimpressed that one of his escorts was damaged unnecessarily.

HMS *ITHURIEL* RAMS THE *COBALTO*, 12 AUGUST 1942 (PP. 44–45)

The ramming of the Italian submarine *Cobalto* (**1**) took place in broad daylight, after two British destroyers had depth-charged and damaged the submarine. As the *Pedestal* convoy moved on to the west, another destroyer, *Ithuriel* (**2**), arrived to take over the attack, as the first two destroyers rejoined the convoy screen. *Ithuriel* was an I-class destroyer built for the Turkish Navy, but was purchased by the Royal Navy in 1939.

Ithuriel hunted for the submarine using her sonar, and when contact was made, she carried out her own depth-charge attack. The crippled Italian submarine was forced to surface due to

buoyancy tank damage, and bobbed up several hundred yards astern of the destroyer. The *Ithuriel*'s skipper promptly spun his ship around and charged at the surfaced submarine, firing her gun at the submarine as she went.

Here we see the *Cobalto* as she is about to be rammed amidships, on her starboard side just behind her damaged conning tower. The collision would make a large dent in the destroyer's bow, but it would also break the pressure hull of the submarine, causing it to sink. Most of the Italian crew would make it off the boat and into the water.

She was spotted from the destroyer *Ithuriel*, which dropped a depth-charge pattern over the submarine. The *Cobalto* was brought to the surface, at which point Lieutenant-Commander David Maitland-Makgill-Crichton turned *Ithuriel* round and rammed the *Cobalto* abaft her conning tower.

Ithuriel's bows were wrecked in the collision, but the submarine was mortally wounded, and sank minutes later. Maitland-Makgill-Crichton had sent a boat to seize the submarine's papers, but she foundered before they could board her and two of the boat crew went down with the submarine. Still, all but two of Cobalto's crew were rescued. *Ithuriel* then rejoined the convoy, driving off an attack by four Stukas on the way at 1749hrs. At that moment, another torpedo spread fired by the Italian submarine *Dandolo* was thwarted by the convoy's zigzag course, and Tenente Campanella's boat was hounded by depth-charge attacks for almost an hour before she escaped. By now the convoy was about 22 miles due north of the Tunisian port of Bizerta. If all went acording to plan, then by around 2300hrs it would pass the Skerki Bank, and enter the Skerki Channel, marking the start of the Narrows. Syfret planned to detach Force Z before then, at around 1915hrs. However, he remained flexible about the timing, as it depended on what happened during the next hour and a half. Significantly, large numbers of enemy aircraft were being detected on radar, forming up 30 miles to the south-east.

These Axis bombers launched their attack at 1830hrs, just as the sun was setting. This time some 98 Italian and German aircraft were involved. In the vanguard were 38 Stukas; nine from the Italian 102° Gruppo, and the rest from Major Martin Mossdorf's I./StG 3. Following behind them

In this photograph, hurriedly taken from the destroyer *Ithuriel* on the afternoon of 12 August, the Italian submarine *Cobalto* is shown settling in the water, where her crew can be seen.

The crew of the Italian submarine *Cobalto*, pictured on the foredeck of the British destroyer *Ithuriel* after their rescue, following *Ithuriel*'s ramming of their submarine. All but two of her crew escaped from the foundering submarine, but a party of British sailors was still on board her when she sank.

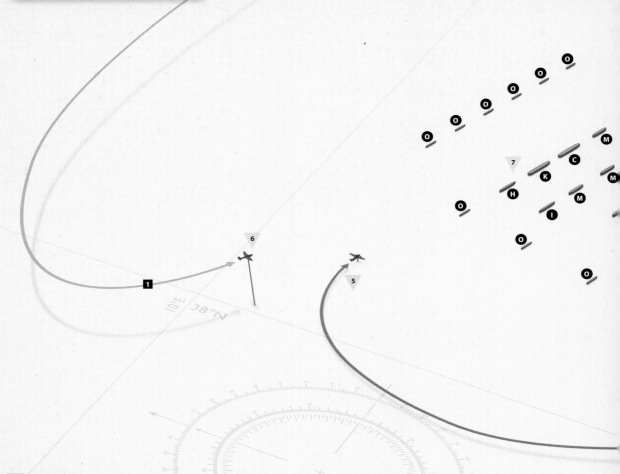

AXIS
1. German I./StG 3 (12 Ju 87 dive-bombers) plus German fighter escorts: eight Me 110s from I./NG 2, 14 Me 109s from II./JG 5
2. Italian 102º Gruppo (nine Ju 87 dive-bombers) plus Italian fighter escorts: eight Cr.42s from 160º Gruppo, 12 Me 202s from 25º Gruppo
3. Italian 132º Gruppo (14 SM.79 and 16 SM.84 torpedo-bombers) plus Italian fighter escorts: 16 Re.2001s from 20º Gruppo

EVENTS

1. British radar detects approximately 100 enemy aircraft massing to the south. Fleet Air Arm fighters from *Indomitable* and *Victorious* are sent to intercept them well away from the convoy. A dogfight ensues, but due to heavy fighter cover the British fighters are unable to break up the attacks. However, the Ju 87s of 102º Gruppo are disrupted, as one dive-bomber is shot down, and three more jettison their bombs and break off the attack.

2. 1835–1840hrs: The remaining five Italian Ju 87 Picchiatello dive-bombers attack *Rodney*. A heavy AA barrage deters two from carrying out their attack, and one Ju 87 is shot down. Two more press home their attacks, but the battleships avoid the bombs – one of which is a near miss off *Rodney*'s port beam.

3. 1836hrs: Seeing the attack develop, Syfret orders his entire force to alter course simultaneously, turning hard to port, to avoid any torpedoes. The new course, held until 1850hrs, is north-north-east.

4. The Italian torpedo bombers of 132º Gruppo divide into two groups. The SM.84s move around the stern of the convoy, to attack it from its port side, while the SM.79s press home an attack directly from the south. At 1843hrs, this southern group launches its torpedoes from an average range of 4,000m. It then continues on over

the convoy before flying off to the north-east. All but one of these torpedoes misses. However, at 1845hrs, one of them hits the destroyer *Foresight*, blowing off her stern.

5. 1845hrs: Approximately half of the SM.84s launch their torpedoes from a similar range, aiming at the carriers. At least six of the bombers jettison their torpedoes to the west of the convoy. The bombers then withdraw to the north. All of these torpedoes miss.

6. 1847hrs: Having circled around the convoy to approach it from the west – the direction of the setting sun – the 12 Ju 87s of I./StG.3 attack the carrier *Indomitable*. The carrier is in her flying-operations position on the port quarter of the convoy. The Stukas remain undetected until they are commencing their attack. Despite a heavy AA barrage, they circle round to strike the carrier from astern with their 250kg bombs.

7. *Indomitable*, weaving at speed, avoids all but two of the bombs directed at her. Some of the near misses, though, damage her lower hull and cause extensive flooding. At 1850hrs, two bombs strike the carrier on her flight deck, near her forward and after lifts. The bombs explode in her hangar deck, causing extensive damage and starting fires. The German Ju 87s then pull off to the north. The fires aboard *Indomitable* are brought under control shortly after 1900hrs.

THE FOURTH AIR ATTACK, 1830–1850HRS, 12 AUGUST 1942

At 1830hrs, the convoy was approximately 325nm north of the Tunisian port of Bizerta, and heading east-south-east, towards the bottleneck of the Skerki Channel. Vice Admiral Syfret planned to withdraw Force Z at 1915hrs, leaving Rear Admiral Burrough and Force X to continue accompanying the convoy through the channel, and the Narrows beyond it. At that moment, enemy aircraft were detected on radar, massing to the south. Force X had its Combat Air Patrol in the air over the convoy, a force of 22 fighters from *Indomitable* and *Victorious*. These were sent to intercept the approaching aircraft, and a dogfight ensued. The bombers, though, were too well protected by fighters for the FAA fighters to disrupt their formations. It soon became apparent that the attackers were concentrating on the British capital ships, rather than the convoy itself. The battleship *Rodney* was dive-bombed by Italian Stukas, while torpedo-bombers targeted the British carriers. The only ship hit, though, was the destroyer *Foresight*, whose stern was broken by an aerial torpedo. Then, unseen, a dozen German Stukas appeared from the west, and dive-bombed the carrier *Indomitable*. She was hit by two bombs, which put her out of action. This, the largest air attack of the *Pedestal* operation, was also one of the most effective.

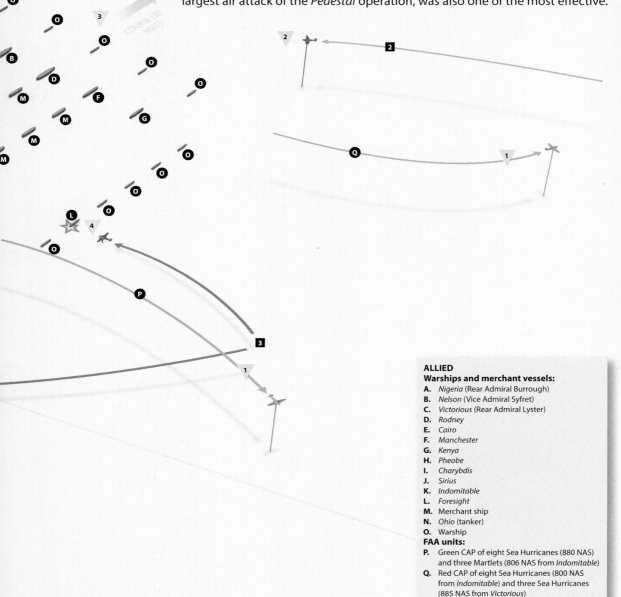

ALLIED
Warships and merchant vessels:
A. *Nigeria* (Rear Admiral Burrough)
B. *Nelson* (Vice Admiral Syfret)
C. *Victorious* (Rear Admiral Lyster)
D. *Rodney*
E. *Cairo*
F. *Manchester*
G. *Kenya*
H. *Pheobe*
I. *Charybdis*
J. *Sirius*
K. *Indomitable*
L. *Foresight*
M. Merchant ship
N. *Ohio* (tanker)
O. Warship
FAA units:
P. Green CAP of eight Sea Hurricanes (880 NAS)
    and three Martlets (806 NAS from *Indomitable*)
Q. Red CAP of eight Sea Hurricanes (800 NAS
    from *Indomitable*) and three Sea Hurricanes
    (885 NAS from *Victorious*)

AIR ATTACK ON *INDOMITABLE*, 12 AUGUST 1942 (PP. 50–51)

This battlescene shows the fleet carrier *Indomitable* (**1**) under attack by Ju 87 Stuka dive-bombers (**2**). Smoke and steam are billowing up around the carrier, as she narrowly avoids several near misses. *Indomitable* has nearly come to a stop, but is still afloat. She is pumping out black smoke from her funnels (**3**), to throw off the German bomb aimers.

The Ju 87 Stukas were all from I./Sturzkampfgeschwader 3, an air group of three squadrons based in Trapani, Sicily. Other aircraft attacked the carrier at the same time. The attack on *Indomitable* began at around 1845hrs, and involved 12 of the air group's Ju 87D and Ju 87R Stukas led by Major Mossdorf, the CO of I./Sturzkampfgeschwader 3. The carrier had been heading east, but began to turn and weave to throw off the aim of the Stuka pilots, who dived from astern of the carrier, approaching from the

west and using the setting sun as cover. The Stukas attacked in batches of three, each following the other as they dropped down in a 70° dive before releasing their 500lb (250kg) SC bombs.

Indomitable was accompanied by a handful of other ships when she was attacked. In the distance, *Phoebe* (**4**) can be seen. *Phoebe* was a Dido-class AA cruiser, with an armament of eight 5.25in. guns in four twin turrets (two forward, two aft), 12 2-pdr (40mm) pom-poms in three quad mounts (one forward, two amidships) and 11 20mm Oerlikon cannons in single mounts (four on her after superstructure, two on the sides of her bridge, two amidships and three at the stern). The carrier and nearby warships have fired off a heavy flak barrage, but *Phoebe* is busy targetting her guns at low-flying Italian SM.79 torpedo-bombers which are attacking to the south.

The carrier *Indomitable* under heavy air attack, at around 1855hrs on 12 August. The carrier has already been hit, and smoke is pouring from the fires in her hangars, while splashes from near misses can be seen astern. Also visible is the AA cruiser *Phoebe*.

were 14 torpedo-armed SM.79s of the 132° Gruppo. The rest of the force consisted of covering fighters, a mixture of Italian and German planes. Their job was to occupy the British fighters while the bombers attacked Lyster's two remaining carriers. Forewarned by radar, though, the British put 22 of *Indomitable*'s Sea Hurricanes into the air to intercept them. A running dogfight followed, but the Axis fighter pilots did their job well, and the bombers were able to press their attack without losing any aircraft.

The first to attack were the torpedo-bombers. Aiming at the two British carriers, they dropped their torpedoes 4,000m away from them, but *Indomitable* and *Victorious* turned hard to port and avoided them. The destroyer *Foresight* wasn't so lucky, and at 1845hrs a torpedo hit her, blowing off her stern. Observers on the *Almeria Lykes* saw sailors catapulted into the air by the blast. There was little hope for the destroyer, but Commander Tyrwhitt of *Tartar* broke formation to do what he could to save her. *Tartar* remained with her while the convoy sailed on, and would do so throughout the long night. Moments later, the Italian Stukas attacked the British battleships. Two aircraft were shot down, and while the rest released their bombs, these all missed. The main attack, though, was still to come.

While these attacks were under way, the Stukas of I./StG 3 flew behind the convoy at 4,000m, using the setting sun to hide their approach. The AA cruiser *Phoebe* was still engaging the torpedo-bombers, and so couldn't react quickly enough to this new threat. The British fighters spotted the Stukas, but it was already too late. A belated barrage of flak erupted around Mossdorf's dive-bombers, but by then they were already dive-bombing *Indomitable*. They attacked in flight-sized groups, and in turn each Stuka released its 250kg bomb at 1,000m before pulling up and turning away. Captain Denis Boyd weaved his ship to dodge the bombs, but he couldn't avoid them all. At 1850hrs two of them struck the carrier's armoured flight deck, penetrating it to explode in the hangar spaces below. The first hit was in front of the forward lift,

Indomitable under attack from German Ju 87 Stukas during the evening of 12 August. Although she was able to avoid most of the bombs, *Indomitable* was hit twice, and effectively put out of action. In this photograph, taken from the cruiser *Phoebe*, she is almost completely obscured by the splashes from near misses.

The destroyer *Foresight* was crippled by an Italian torpedo during the attack on the evening of 12 August that put the carrier *Indomitable* out of action. The stern was blown off the destroyer, but she remained afloat until the following morning. This photograph was taken from the destroyer *Tartar*.

wrecking it and causing mayhem in the hangar below. The explosion ignited aviation fuel, and the resulting fire set off ammunition for the forward 4.5in. guns. It took some 40 minutes to bring the raging fire under control.

The second bomb penetrated the flight deck amidships, just behind the after lift. It exploded in the after hangar, the blast blowing a large hole in the after flight deck and wrecking the hangar sides. This meant *Indomitable*'s flight deck was now completely out of action. Also, one of the near misses off the ship's port side damaged the ship's hull plates, causing extensive flooding. Some 760 tons of water poured into the ship, which began listing to port. A second near miss damaged the port-side pom-pom batteries amidships. Their job done, the Stukas then climbed away, pursued by fire from the convoy. Then, *Indomitable*'s damage-control teams began the gruelling task of saving their ship.

Twenty miles to the south, off the Galite Islands, the damaged merchantman *Deucalion* was steering towards the coast, shepherded by *Bramham*. Captain Brown of *Deucalion* hoped to skirt it until they were past the Narrows. At 1946hrs *Deucalion* was attacked by two Ju 88s, but Brown avoided the bombs. Then, at 2120hrs they were attacked again. This time they were five miles offshore, near the Cani Islands. Suddenly, two He 111 torpedo-bombers appeared to the south. They were gliding in with their engines cut, and in the darkness they weren't spotted until it was too late. Restarting their engines, the bombers then attacked *Deucalion* from either beam. Moments later, a torpedo struck the ship's starboard quarter, the detonation igniting her cargo of aviation fuel.

The two bombs which struck *Indomitable* that evening penetrated her armoured flight deck to explode inside her hangar. They also ripped holes in her deck and the hangar sides, and put both her lifts out of action. Fortunately, her fighters involved in the air battle overhead were able to land on *Victorious*.

A poor quality photograph, taken during an air attack by Ju 88s a little after noon on 12 August, showing the SS *Deucalion* under attack. Moments later, the merchant ship was hit by bombs dropped from another Ju 88, and flooding damaged her engines, which meant she had to be left behind by the convoy.

Captain Brown immediately gave the order to abandon ship. *Bramham* rescued the survivors, then finished off *Deucalion* with depth charges before heading off in search of the convoy.

The convoy was re-formed after the air attack, and continued to the east-south-east, making 16 knots. Syfret had planned to withdraw Force Z at around 1915hrs, when the convoy was approaching the Skerki Bank. This was an area of shallows, reefs and shoals lying due north of Tunis, and west of Sicily. It also marked the start of the Narrows. At 1855hrs *Indomitable* had been ordered to return to Gibraltar, protected by *Charybdis* and the destroyers *Lightning*, *Lookout* and *Somali*. Her aircraft all landed safely on *Victorious*. By then, *Rodney* had developed a faulty boiler which reduced her speed. So, at 1900hrs, a little ahead of schedule, Syfret ordered Force Z to part company with the convoy. Rear Admiral Burrough was now in charge of the convoy's protection.

Sunset that evening was still 90 minutes away, and Burrough fully expected more attacks before dark. So, as they approached the Skerki Channel, the passage between Skerki Bank and the Tunisian coast, he re-formed the convoy into two columns. The three minesweeping destroyers *Fury*, *Icarus* and *Intrepid* also moved ahead of the convoy and streamed their minesweeping gear, in case mines were encountered in the narrow channel. The Skerki Channel was also a perfect ambush spot for submarines. Sure enough, Tenente Scandola's boat *Dessiè* was lying in wait. At 1937hrs, the reorganization of the convoy was still under way when he fired off four

The Italian Adua-class submarine *Axum*, launched in 1936, was one of the boats deployed in the Skerki Channel between Sicily and Tunisia to attack the *Pedestal* convoy. Late on 12 August, her commander, Tenente Ferrini made one of the most successful submarine attacks of the war, sinking one British cruiser and damaging a tanker and another cruiser.

SUBMARINE ATTACKS IN THE SKERKI CHANNEL, 1945–2015HRS, 12 AUGUST 1942

At 1900hrs, Force Z left the convoy, leaving Rear Admiral Burrough and his Force X to escort the convoy through the Skerki Channel, and on to Malta. The channel was a bottleneck, and so as he approached it, Burrough reorganized his convoy into a narrower formation. This process was still under way when they were attacked by an Italian submarine. Its spread of torpedoes missed, but minutes later another spread, fired from

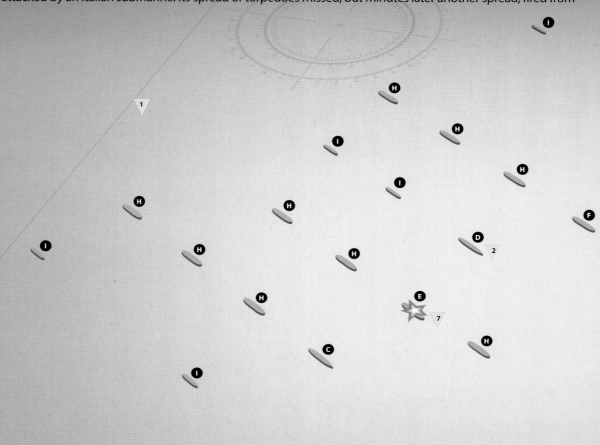

the submarine *Axum*, were much more effective. Approaching the convoy from the north-east, the boat's commander Tenente Ferrini drew close to the outer screen of escorts, and then, at 1955hrs, launched four torpedoes. After a run of just over a minute, the first of them hit the port side of Burrough's flagship *Nigeria*, 1,300m away to the south. Half a minute later, two more torpedoes struck the port side of the AA cruiser *Cairo*, 500m beyond *Nigeria*. Then, at 1959hrs, the last torpedo struck the port quarter of the tanker *Ohio* – the most valuable ship in the convoy. *Cairo* sank within 15 minutes, while *Nigeria* was crippled in the attack, and was forced to return to Gibraltar. *Ohio*, although damaged, continued to limp on towards Malta.

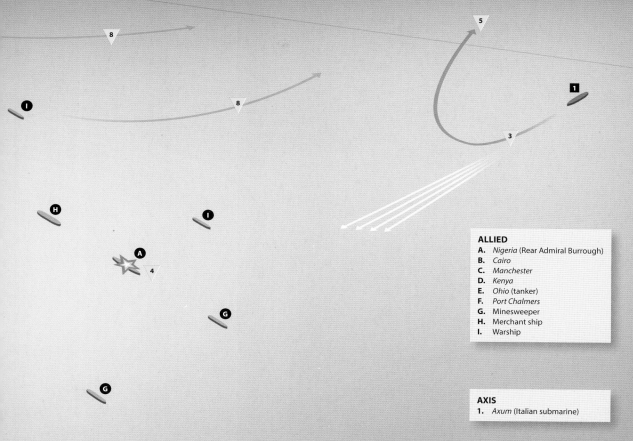

ALLIED

A. *Nigeria* (Rear Admiral Burrough)
B. *Cairo*
C. *Manchester*
D. *Kenya*
E. *Ohio* (tanker)
F. *Port Chalmers*
G. Minesweeper
H. Merchant ship
I. Warship

AXIS

1. *Axum* (Italian submarine)

▼ EVENTS

1. 1937hrs: The Italian submarine *Dessiè* fires a spread of four torpedoes at the convoy, but no hits are made. The convoy continues on its way without detecting the submarine.

2. From 1900hrs onwards, when Force Z breaks off from the convoy, Rear Admiral Burrough in his flagship *Nigeria* reorders his convoy into a tighter formation. By 1955hrs, he has reduced the spacing between the convoy columns to 500 yards (2.5 cables), with the same distance between the ships within the column. After 2000hrs, he plans to then form two convoy columns for the passage through the Narrows. He also reorganizes the escorts; the light cruiser *Kenya*, followed by two escorts, steams through the convoy to take station ahead of the convoy's third column, while the escorts are to move ahead of the convoy.

3. 1955hrs: Spotting this cluster of ships passing him to the south-west, Tenente Ferrini in *Axum* fires a salvo of four 53.3cm torpedoes at the convoy. The nearest major warship, *Nigeria*, is 1,300m away, which means the torpedoes have a running time of 63 seconds.

4. 1957hrs: a torpedo strikes *Nigeria* in her port side, just below the bridge. The explosion rips a hole in the cruiser's side, knocking out her forward boiler rooms. As she floods, she begins listing heavily to port. In all, 52 of her crew are killed in the attack.

5. As soon as he fires his torpedoes, Ferrini dives his boat and turns her away to the north, then the north-west, as he expects to be counter-attacked by the British escorts. As they dive, his crew hear a succession of four explosions as their torpedoes detonate.

6. 1958hrs: Two torpedoes strike the port quarter of the AA cruiser *Cairo*. Her stern is blown off by the explosion, and her after hull floods rapidly, which raises her bows out of the water. Having lost power she comes to a stop, and begins sinking. A total of 25 of her crew are killed. The destroyer *Pathfinder* comes alongside to rescue the survivors, and *Cairo* sinks at 2015hrs, having been scuttled by a torpedo fired from the escort destroyer *Derwent*.

7. 1959hrs: The fourth torpedo fired by *Axum* strikes the port side of the tanker *Ohio*, in the third column of the convoy. The detonation ignites some of the aviation fuel she carries, and the resulting fireball reaches as high as the tanker's masthead. Captain Mason of *Ohio* abandons the engine room, and has his men fight the fire before it spreads into the ship's other storage tanks.

8. As soon as *Nigeria* is hit, the escort destroyers *Penn* and *Derwent* search for the submarine, and carry out depth-charge attacks a mile to the north of the convoy. *Axum*, though, avoids these, and makes good her escape.

9. 2000hrs: As it becomes clear that his flagship is crippled, Burrough signals the destroyer *Ashanti*, on the starboard side of the convoy, to come alongside. He will transfer to her, while *Nigeria* will be sent back to Gibraltar, protected by a small escort.

The SS *Ohio* is struck by a torpedo fired by the submarine *Axum* on the evening of 12 August. Behind her are the merchantmen SS *Port Chalmers* and SS *Melbourne Star*, both in the adjacent column of the convoy. The photograph was taken from the cruiser *Manchester*. Just ahead of the *Port Chalmers* was the cruiser *Cairo*, which was sunk by two torpedoes from the same salvo.

torpedoes, but these all missed. However, a little to the east was Tenente Ferrini's boat *Axum*. The *Axum* was to the north-east of the convoy, and as he crept closer to it, he monitored the reordering of the convoy. At 1955hrs, when he saw what appeared to be a cluster of ships in his periscope, he fired four torpedoes.

It was probably the most perfect submarine attack of the war. The range to the nearest vessel was around 1,300m. After 63 seconds Ferrini heard a detonation, followed by others. Ferrini thought he'd hit a British cruiser and possibly another warship. In fact, he'd been much more successful. The first of his torpedoes struck the port side of Burrough's flagship *Nigeria*, detonating below her bridge, ripping a hole in her hull. Her forward boiler rooms flooded, and the cruiser began listing to port. Captain Stuart Paton isolated the flooding, and counterflooded to reduce the list, but his cruiser had been disabled, and 52 of his crew killed.

The AA cruiser *Cairo* was then struck by two torpedoes on her starboard quarter. These blew her stern off and she slewed to a stop, her bows rising out of the water as the stern of the cruiser flooded. In all, 23 of her crew were killed. Moments later, at 1957hrs, and half a mile off *Cairo*'s starboard quarter, Ferrini's last torpedo struck the tanker *Ohio* on her port side, blowing a large hole in her hull. As some of her fuel ignited, a column of fire reached as high as the masthead. Captain Dudley Mason ordered his men up from the engine room, while his crew did what they could to fight the blaze. The heat, though, was so intense it could be felt by ships a mile away.

Bicester, *Penn* and *Derwent* broke off from the convoy to hunt for *Axum* and drop depth charges, but Ferrini was sensibly already making his escape. On board the *Ohio* flooding helped douse the flames, and the blaze was gradually brought under control. It helped that the fuel had been stowed in oil drums, rather than filled straight into the ship's tanks. So, *Ohio*, escorted by *Ledbury*, was able to limp on. Now, though, not only had the convoy become disordered, but with *Nigeria* disabled it had lost one of its largest escorts.

By 2015hrs the destroyer *Ashanti* had come alongside *Nigeria*, and Burrough transferred into Captain Onslow's destroyer. He then ordered *Nigeria* back to Gibraltar, accompanied by *Bicester* and *Wilton*. There was no hope for *Cairo*, though, and Captain Cecil Hardy evacuated his crew into the *Pathfinder*. At 2015hrs the cruiser was sunk by one of *Derwent*'s torpedoes. By sunset, the convoy was spread out, its ships illuminated by the blaze from *Ohio*. At that critical point, as the sun was disappearing, yet more enemy aircraft were detected, approaching from the north-east.

This fourth air attack was carried out by 30 Ju 88s from I./KG 54 and II./KG 57, accompanied by seven torpedo-armed He 111s from II./KG 76, and six fighters. They struck at 2035hrs, as the convoy was trying to re-form. One of the first of the bombs narrowly missed *Ashanti*, causing a fire aft. A torpedo dropped by a Heinkel narrowly missed *Icarus*, but it soon became clear that the real targets were the merchant ships. Force Z threw up an AA barrage, and *Penn* laid funnel smoke to screen some of the merchantmen, but it wasn't enough. For the next half hour, the Germans tore the convoy apart.

The first victim was the SS *Brisbane Star*, which was struck in the bow by a torpedo dropped from a Heinkel. The explosion blew a hole through the ship's bow, causing flooding. Unable now to keep up with the convoy, Captain Neville Riley set a course for the coast, which he planned to hug until dawn. Astern of her, the SS *Empire Hope* was targeted by Ju 88s. Captain G. Williams dodged 18 bombs, but then his luck ran out. A near miss blew a 15ft hole in her hull, water poured into her machinery spaces, and the *Empire Hope* was left dead in the water. She was now a sitting duck. Then, at 2050hrs she took two direct hits to her after hold. It held fuel and explosives, and as the fire raged, Williams had no alternative but to abandon ship. As the crew of *Empire Hope* jumped over the side into the sea, now covered in a layer of burning oil, more bombers attacked the SS *Clan Ferguson*, on the port side of the convoy. *Kenya*'s pom-pom gunners hit one of the attackers, but the passenger liner was struck at 2102hrs, and torn apart.

As an observer in *Kenya* recalled: 'One moment there was this fine vessel, the next a huge atomic-like explosion and she had gone, dissapeared with just a blueish ring of flame on the water and a mushroom of smoke and flame thousands of feet in the air.' Like *Empire Hope*, the *Clan Ferguson* had been carrying aviation fuel and ammunition. In fact, the bombers probably weren't responsible for the ship's death blow. That came from a torpedo dropped from an He 111, which struck the ship's port quarter seconds before the bombs hit. This detonated the ammunition stowed in her after hold. Also, the *Clan Ferguson* didn't sink immediately. Her half-submerged wreck remained afloat until midnight, allowing 64 of her crew to escape from her.

The torpedo fired by the Italian submarine *Axum* crippled Burrough's flagship, the light cruiser *Nigeria*. After the Force X commander transferred to *Ashanti*, the badly damaged and listing *Nigeria* was sent back to Gibraltar, screened by destroyers.

The loss of these two merchant ships was a major blow. The only consolation was that it was later claimed that two of the German bombers were flying over the *Clan Ferguson* when she exploded, and were torn apart by the blast. As always, the ships in the convoy were under orders not to stop and help. Their job was to press on to Malta, regardless of what happened around them. In this case, most of the survivors weren't even picked up by the escorts, who missed them in the darkness. Instead they were rescued by the enemy, and so became prisoners of war.

Reacting to the loss of so many of his charges, Commodore Arthur Venables in the SS *Port Chalmers* briefly turned around and headed back to the west, followed by three merchantmen. This added to the disorder within the convoy. Venables was right to be alarmed. As the aircraft flew off, nearby submarines were drawn to the burning merchantmen, and closed in. One of these was the *Alagi*, commanded by Tenente Puccini. At 2112hrs, he fired four torpedoes at the convoy, which was emerging from the south-eastern end of the channel, preceded by the minesweepers. A lookout on *Kenya* spotted the tracks, and Captain Russell turned the cruiser hard over to avoid them. All but one of them missed. The last one struck *Kenya*'s bow, causing heavy flooding forward. Three of her crew were also killed. The damage, though, wasn't severe enough to prevent *Kenya* from keeping up with the convoy. *Alagi* escaped after a depth-charging by *Ashanti* and *Pathfinder*.

Some 80 miles to the west, Syfret heard of the attack, and ordered the AA cruiser *Charybdis* and the destroyers *Eskimo* and *Somali* to reinforce Force X. So, by 2300hrs the bulk of Syfret's Force Z was to the north of the Galite Islands, heading west, with the damaged *Nigeria* and her escorts following astern. *Charybdis* with two destroyers was speeding east, while the bulk of the *Pedestal* convoy and Force X were to the south-east, approaching Cape Bon. Burrough's next problem was reforming his convoy, so he sent *Pathfinder* off to round up stragglers. By then, the merchantmen were spread over a dozen miles of sea. At the rear was *Ohio* and *Ledbury*, the tanker

The light cruiser *Kenya*, pictured under air attack on 12 August. A stick of bombs has fallen astern of her as she begins to turn to starboard, to throw off the aim of another bomber. In the background, further south, other ships of the convoy can be seen under attack.

Situation: evening, 12 August 1942

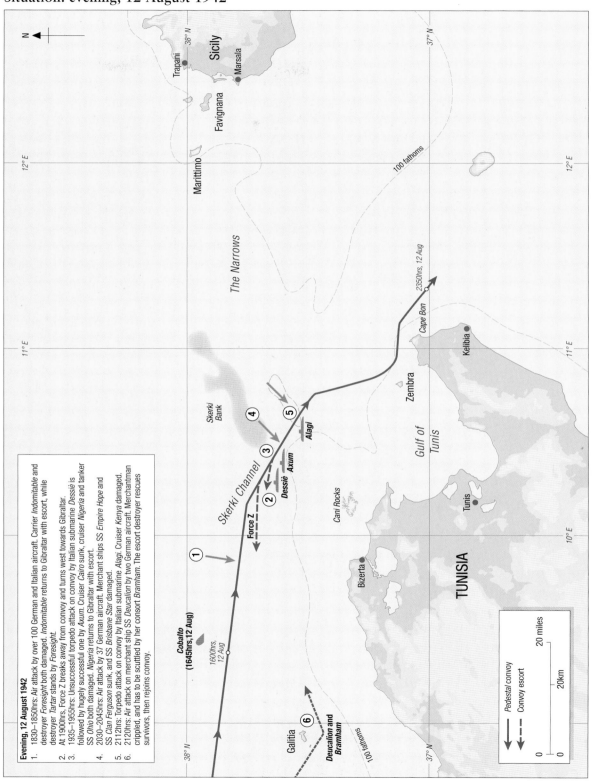

Evening, 12 August 1942

1. 1830–1850hrs: Air attack by over 100 German and Italian aircraft. Carrier *Indomitable* and destroyer *Foresight* both damaged. *Indomitable* returns to Gibraltar with escort, while destroyer *Tartar* stands by *Foresight*.
2. At 1900hrs, Force Z breaks away from convoy and turns west towards Gibraltar.
3. 1935–1955hrs: Unsuccessful torpedo attack on convoy by Italian submarine *Dessiè* is followed by hugely successful one by *Axum*. Cruiser *Cairo* sunk, cruiser *Nigeria* and tanker SS *Ohio* both damaged. *Nigeria* returns to Gibraltar with escort.
4. 2030–2045hrs: Air attack by 37 German aircraft. Merchant ships SS *Empire Hope* and SS *Clan Ferguson* sunk, and SS *Brisbane Star* damaged.
5. 2112hrs: Torpedo attack on convoy by Italian submarine *Alagi*. Cruiser *Kenya* damaged.
6. 2120hrs: Air attack on merchant ship SS *Deucalion* by two German aircraft. Merchantman crippled, and has to be scuttled by her consort *Bramham*. The escort destroyer rescues survivors, then rejoins convoy.

being the most precious of Burrough's charges. *Brisbane Star* was to the south-west of the other ships, on her own in the Bay of Tunis. The escort destroyer *Bramham*, carrying the survivors of the *Deucalion*, had rejoined the convoy. All Burrough could really do, though, was wait for the stragglers to catch up.

The rounding up of the convoy took time. At 2330hrs *Ohio* and *Ledbury* passed the flaming wreck of the *Clan Ferguson*, surrounded by a burning slick of oil. Somewhere ahead of them the merchant ships *Almeria Lykes*, *Wairangi* and *Waimarama* had formed their own column, and were reunited with the remnants of the convoy a little before midnight. That gave Burrough, still aboard *Tartar*, some chance of protecting his charges. The need for this was highlighted at 2348hrs, when an explosion erupted a few miles astern. This was the Italian submarine *Bronzo*, performing a mercy killing of the *Clan Ferguson*, which was finished off with a single torpedo. Had Tenente Buldrini spotted the *Ohio* limp by 20 minutes earlier, the outcome of *Pedestal* might have been very different.

By midnight the head of the convoy was off Cape Bon, and six miles offshore. This marked the end of the Narrows. Once past it, their route took them down the coast as far as the small Tunisian port of Kelibia. Then it turned east towards Malta. By dawn, six and a half hours away, Burrough expected air cover from Malta would appear. All he had to do was to keep the *Pedestal* convoy safe until then. What he didn't realize was that beyond Cape Bon two dozen enemy MTBs were lying in wait. The long night was far from over.

THE NIGHT ACTION, 12/13 AUGUST

Once past Cape Bon, the three minesweeping destroyers continued on down the coast. This group, led by Commander Charles Kitcat in *Intrepid*, was vital to the success of the operation, as these waters, together with those around Malta, had been extensively mined by the enemy. Then, at 0040hrs, *Icarus* on the port side of the group detected small contacts on her radar. Lurking to the east were the four boats of the Italian 18th MAS Division. After kick-starting their engines, the boats roared in and unleashed a four-torpedo salvo. They were met by heavy fire from Kitcat's destroyers, who turned hard to port to avoid the torpedoes. All of them missed, but two of the destroyer minesweeper's sets of parvanes were swept away. Tenente Perasso's MAS boats then broke off the attack under cover of a smokescreen, and withdrew back out to sea. One of them later claimed a hit.

This, though, was only the start of the assault. Similar attacks would continue until dawn. While the convoy and its escorts were reasonably well provided with AA weapons, these were less effective against small surface targets, as the guns couldn't depress far enough to engage them. Even radar was less effective, as these small wooden-built boats were hard to detect. The next assault came at 0050hrs, as the middle part of the straggling convoy passed within four miles of Cape Bon. The lighthouse there was still operating, and its light shone for miles, sweeping over the ships as they passed by. This suited Kapitänleutnant Friedrich Kemnade commanding the German 3rd S-Boat Flotilla. He attacked with three boats, but when *S-58* was badly shot up, the attackers launched their torpedoes and withdrew. No hits

The damage control parties and injured crewmen of the cruiser *Manchester*, after their ship was torpedoed in July 1941. In August 1942, these men were less fortunate, and despite similar efforts they were unable to save their ship.

were scored. Meanwhile, some 14.5km to the north, Oberleutnant Albert Müller commanding *S-59* had lost contact with the rest of his flotilla. So, he carried out his own unsuccessful torpedo run on an unidentified straggler. Later, on his return to his base at Port Empedocle in Sicily, Müller claimed to have sunk a 15,000-ton tanker.

By 0100hrs, Kitcat's minesweepers were 20 miles to the south-south-east, and about five miles off the coast, abreast of Kelibia. That April, the destroyer *Havock* had run aground off Sidi Mansour headland, two miles north of the port. Now the beached destroyer was used as a hiding place for the six boats of the Italian 2nd MS Boat Division. There, Capitano di Corvetta Giorgio Manuti watched the minesweepers pass by, then spotted a light cruiser following them, followed by two merchant ships. On Manuti's orders, the hidden MS boats started their engines and roared into battle. Manuti in *MS-16*, followed by Tenente Mezzadra in *MS-22*, approached the cruiser from the landward side, while the remaining boats raced east to fall upon the convoy from seaward.

TORPEDOING THE *MANCHESTER*, 13 AUGUST 1942 (PP. 64–65)

At 0030hrs on 13 August, the convoy was attacked by small groups of German E-boats and Italian motor torpedo boats (known as MS boats). At that point the convoy escort had been reduced to the cruisers and destroyers earmarked to accompany it through to Malta. The others, including the battleships and carriers, had turned back at the mouth of the Narrows, the constricted water between Sicily and Tunisia.

The waters to the east of the Narrows were likely to be mined, so the convoy redeployed into a two-column formation where the minesweepers led the way, followed by a group of warships, then the merchantmen, with another group of warships bringing up the rear. However, due to earlier attacks by submarines, the convoy had straggled somewhat, and was now bunched into groups of ships rather than two neat columns.

At 0030hrs the escorts picked up blips on radar – the enemy torpedo boats, who headed in to attack. The German boats led the way, but scored no hits. Then, as the convoy was passing Kelibia on the Tunisian coast (just to the south-east of Cape Bon and east-north-east of Tunis), the bulk of the Italian boats attacked. Some of these were driven off by heavy fire from the escorts, but a few made it through. The Kelibia lighthouse, with its clockwise revolving light, illuminated the sea – and the convoy – for several miles.

At 0107hrs two Italian motor torpedo boats, *MS-16* and *MS-22*, managed to creep close to the convoy without being detected. They reached a perfect firing position just as the light cruiser *Manchester* appeared, some 500 yards to the north. The two Italian skippers kick-started their engines and roared in to make a torpedo

attack. They were spotted, and Captain Drew of the *Manchester* turned towards them, to reduce the target he presented. All his forward 6in. guns (two turrets of three guns each) opened fire on the boats, firing in salvoes, which missed – but only just.

MS-16 launched her port 21in. torpedo, while *MS-22* snap-fired both of hers. One of the three torpedoes – probably the one from the right-hand boat, *MS-16* – struck the starboard quarter of the fast-moving cruiser and detonated. The Italian boats then spun around and escaped into the darkness. The blast flooded the port and starboard engine room and the after boiler room, and cut electrical power. Steam escaped, and parts of the engine room caught fire. Flooding spread too, and the ship settled slightly by the stern and slewed round to starboard, her rudders either not answering or jammed.

Astern of the cruiser, the American SS *Almeria Lykes* (a 7,773-ton US-built Type C3 cargo ship) loomed out of the darkness, on the same course as the *Manchester*, having turned to starboard too. She was now on a collision course, so she turned hard to port and moved out of the way. Astern of her another merchantman, the *Glenorchy*, was also off the *Almeria Lykes'* port quarter, and had to alter to port too, to avoid being rammed by the American freighter.

Shown here is the moment the torpedo struck the *Manchester* (**1**), causing a huge plume of water in front of the Town-class light cruiser. In the foreground *MS-16* (**2**) is turning away and escaping. Astern of *Manchester*, the *Almeria Lykes* (**3**) can be seen.

Later that morning *Manchester* had to be abandoned and scuttled by other British warships.

On board the cruiser *Manchester*, Manuti's two boats were only spotted when they were less than half a mile away. The Italians had another advantage, as *Manchester* and the merchantmen *Almeria Lykes* and *Glenorchy* behind her were illuminated by the beam of the Kelibia lighthouse, perched on top of an old fort above the port's entrance. Manuti launched his port torpedo at 0104hrs at a range of just 800m. It proved faulty, though, and veered harmlessly off course. Captain Harold Drew turned *Manchester* to port to comb the torpedo tracks, his forward 6in. guns firing at the approaching enemy boats. It was too late, though. At 0106hrs, from a range of just 750m, Mezzadra launched his own two torpedoes. Some 50 seconds later, one or possibly both of them struck *Manchester* on her starboard quarter.

The light cruiser *Manchester*, pictured engaging Italian motor torpedo boats off Kelibia during the early hours of 13 August. Moments later she was immobilized by a torpedo hit to her starboard side. Later that night the cruiser was scuttled by her crew.

This blew a hole in her side and water flooded into her machinery spaces. *Manchester* lost all electrical power, and she began to list to starboard. Damage-control teams struggled to contain the flooding and rescue the engine room staff. The port outer shaft kept spinning, though, and the ship turned in a lazy half circle before the way came off her. By this time the two torpedo boats had sped off, while the rest of Manuti's force ignored the stricken cruiser, as they looked for other targets. For the moment, *Manchester* was safe. Half a mile behind, the American merchantman *Almeria Lykes* turned and headed seaward at full speed, regardless of the risk of mines. Meanwhile, the *Glenorchy* turned south, to slip past *Manchester* to follow the minesweepers. Behind her, another merchantman, the *Waimarama*, continued on after the *Glenorchy*.

After that, due to the dispersement of the convoy, *Manchester* and her crew were left alone and drifting. By 0130hrs, Drew and his crew managed to stabilize the ship by counterflooding, which reduced her starboard list to just 5 degrees. She was still without full power, although Drew managed to transmit a brief report to Burrough in *Ashanti*. Further to the north, Burrough sent *Pathfinder* surging ahead to protect *Manchester*. The destroyer had been escorting *Dorset* and *Melbourne Star*, so they were temporarily left on their own. When *Pathfinder* reached *Manchester* at 0140hrs, Drew was confident that the cruiser could be saved. However, he asked Commander Edwards Gibbs of *Pathfinder* to transfer 158 of the cruiser's non-essential crew to the destroyer, before *Pathfinder* turned back north again to rejoin Burrough. Meanwhile, Captain William Henderson of the *Almeria Lykes* spotted mines, and turned back south, eventually rejoining Kitcat's minesweepers.

Six minutes after *Manchester* was hit, the SS *Rochester Castle*, five miles to the north-east of Kelibia, was steaming south behind *Dorset* when another Italian MS boat appeared off her port beam. It was the *MS-26*, one of Manuti's squadron. *MS-26* fired a single torpedo that struck *Rochester Castle* amidships, blowing a hole in the port side of No. 3 hold. Captain

Richard Wren and his crew were eventually able to contain the flooding, and kept going, making 13 knots. A mile to the south, another Italian MS boat cut across the bow of *Dorset*, and instinctively Captain Jack Tuckett tried to ram the speeding craft. The MS boat evaded this manoeuvre with feet to spare, and disappeared towards the coast.

With that, Tuckett decided that the risk of further attacks was too great. He turned to port, onto a course which would take him to the north of Pantelleria. Captain Wren of *Rochester Castle* reached the same conclusion, and followed *Dorset* around to the north-east. After that, apart from a flurry when *Glenorchy* exchanged fire with a passing Italian MAS boat, there was a brief lull in the attacks. During this pause, the badly scattered convoy continued on its way, either continuing on past the stricken *Manchester* or else following Kitcat's minesweepers. In accordance with his orders, once south of the Kelibia light, Kitcat turned south-east, and began clearing the path the convoy had intended to take through the Italian minefield, keeping well to the south of Pantelleria.

It was now almost 0200hrs. Burrough in *Ashanti* was off Kelibia, having exchanged signals with Drew of *Manchester* earlier. Drew assured Burrough he expected to get under way shortly. Further to the south-east, between Burrough and Kitcat, were several merchant ships and two escorts. Ten minutes earlier, *Glenorchy* had fired at an Italian torpedo boat, which vanished again. Suddenly, a searchlight came on, illuminating the merchantman. It came from Tenente Calvani's *MS-31*, one of Manuti's boats. Captain George Leslie turned *Glenorchy* towards the light, which was quickly switched off. Then, without warning, two torpedoes struck the merchant ship's port quarter. It was a death blow. The hull was ripped open, and six engine room staff were killed in the twin explosions. The

The young crew of one of *Manchester*'s pom-pom AA mounts, during a training exercise. This reflects the age of most of her ship's company. The two sailors in the centre are operating the elevating and firing levers, while the trainer stands on the right.

merchantman began listing heavily as water flooded into her. Leslie quickly gave the order to abandon ship.

The survivors launched the undamaged rafts and lifeboats, but Leslie stayed aboard as his burning ship sank beneath him. The crew made it to shore four miles away, some of them towed there by Calvani. They were duly taken prisoner by the Vichy French police. This would be the fate of many of the merchant crews that night. While some were rescued by British warships or were lost, others made it ashore and were interned, while others were rescued by Axis seaplanes or boats, and became prisoners of war.

Meanwhile, *Manchester* was still dead in the water, six miles north-east of Kelibia. All attempts to get her moving had failed, and so at 0250hrs Captain Drew gave the order to rig scuttling charges, and then abandon ship. This was achieved without fuss, and with his crew safely off, the charges were fired at 0315hrs. Ironically, by then the chief engineer had managed to restore power to an engine, but the scuttling charges were already set and couldn't be deactivated. Still, even after they detonated, *Manchester* stubbornly remained afloat, and would remain so until dawn. Meanwhile, some of the ship's boats made for the shore. There, over 500 of her crew were taken prisoner by the French, and were eventually taken to the Laghouat prison camp in the Algerian desert. They were freed that November, when the camp was liberated by the US Army. Another 321 crewmen were rescued by friendly destroyers, either *Pathfinder*, *Somali* or *Eskimo*.

Just after 0200hrs Sottotenente Bencini in *MS-26* was 11km south of Kelibia when he spotted a merchant ship and a destroyer – *Almeria Lykes* and *Pathfinder*. He tried to creep closer, but was suddenly illuminated by a starshell, then raked with gunfire. Just as he broke away, he spotted a British cruiser beyond the two ships. He launched two torpedoes at her, but both missed. Bencini then turned away and ran towards the coast, laying smoke and dropping depth charges to screen his withdrawal. Two more boats, Tenente Le Para's *MS-25* and Sottotenente Patrone's *MS-23*, were close by, but the cruiser *Kenya* drove them off with her 6in. guns. However, Tenente Calvani of *MS-31* was more circumspect. Rather than attack the ships, he shadowed them throughout the night, sending sighting reports back to Manuti.

There was now another lull in the battle. This was particularly welcome to Burrough, who was still trying to reassemble his battered convoy. Ahead of him Kitcat reported that they had now passed through the minefield, but that *Fury* and *Icarus* had lost their minseweeping paravanes, while *Icarus* only had one of her two sweeps left. Still, they had reached open water. Then, shortly before 0300hrs, Burrough was relieved to see *Charybdis*, *Eskimo* and *Somali* come up astern of him. By then, after conferring with Captain George Voelcker of *Charybdis*, he had a better understanding of where some of his ships were. The *Pedestal* convoy was still strung out, with its head some 25 miles south-east of Kelibia, and its tail just five miles off the Tunisian coast.

Behind Kitcat's three minesweeper destroyers were *Kenya* and *Pathfinder*, in sight of the merchantmen *Santa Elisa* and *Wairangi*. Further astern of them were *Almeria Lykes*, *Port Chalmers* and *Melbourne* Star, followed by *Waimarama*, together with the escort destroyers *Bramham* and *Penn*. Behind them came *Ashanti* and the three reinforcements. The convoy was scattered in a long swath of ocean to the south-west of Pantelleria. Even if they survived the night, unless the ships could be brought together they would be easy prey for Axis aircraft when day broke.

MTB ATTACK, 0040–0115HRS, 13 AUGUST 1942

After passing Cape Bon around midnight, the convoy continued down the Tunisian coast past Kelibia. Ahead of it, Commander Kitcat's minesweeper-destroyers cleared a path through the enemy minefield. Then, from 0040hrs on, the now very strung-out convoy was subjected to a series of attacks by small groups of Axis MTBs, of the Italian 18th MAS Division and 2nd MS Division, and the German 3rd S-Boat Flotilla. These initial attacks lasted less than half an hour, but they proved to be only the start of a running battle with these torpedo boats which would continue until dawn.

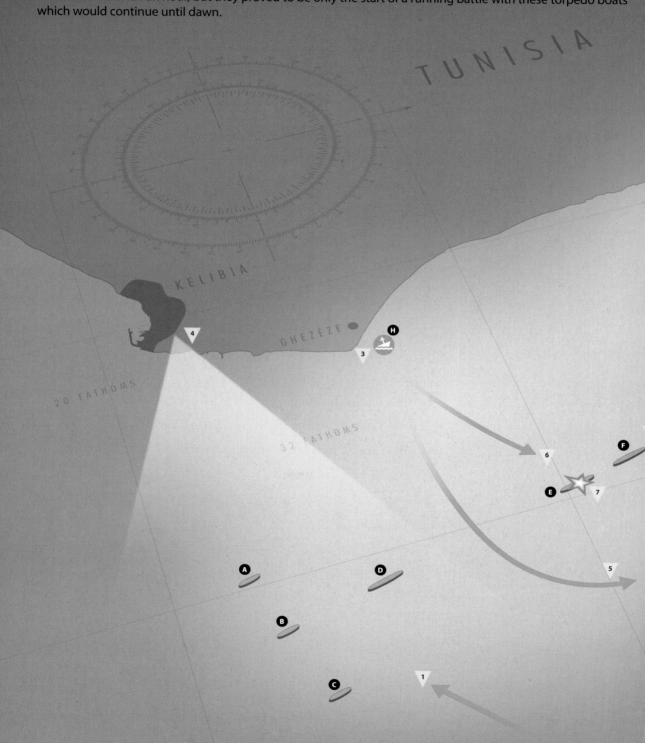

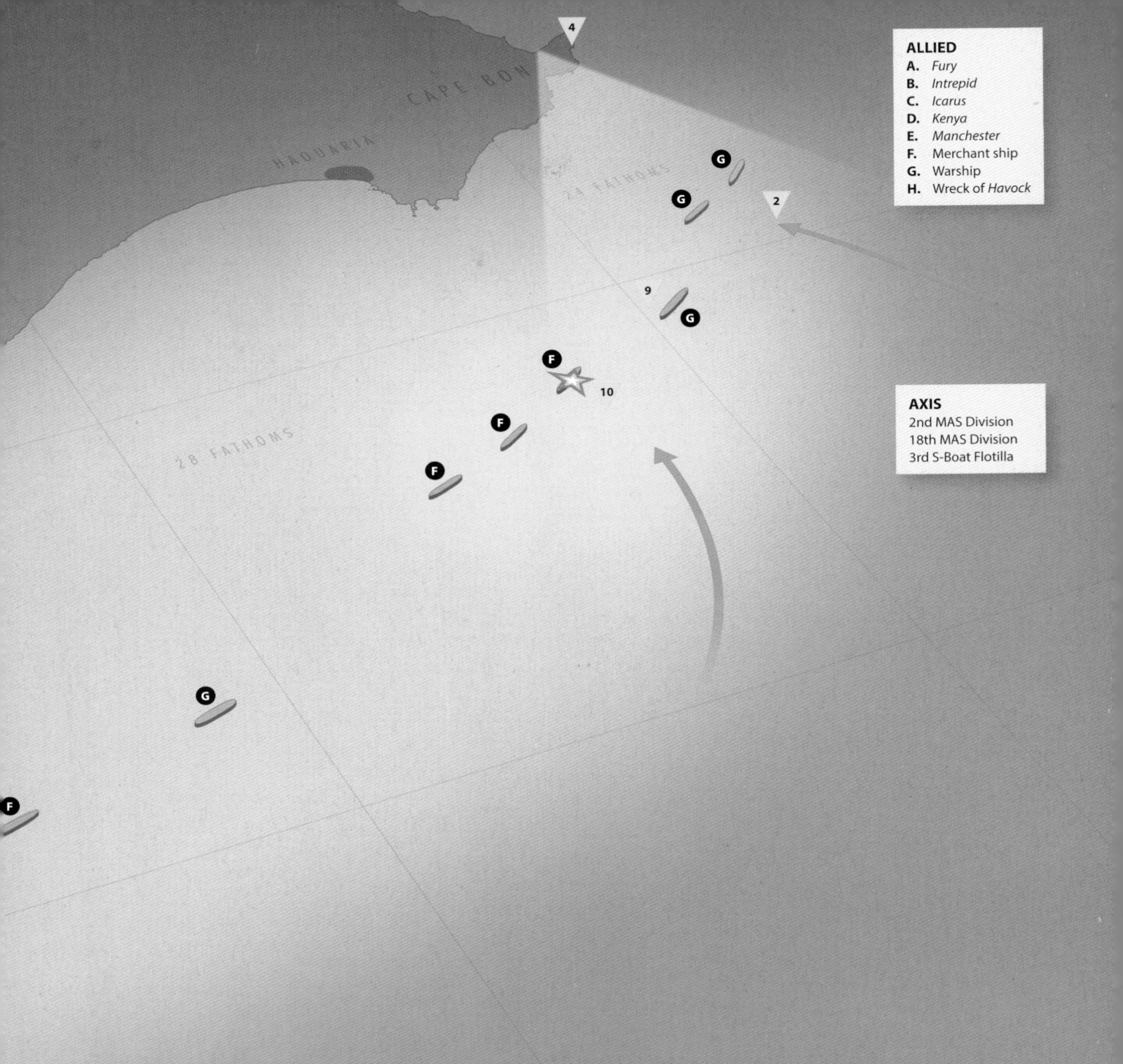

4

CAPE BON

HAOUARIA

24 FATHOMS

2

9

10

28 FATHOMS

▼ EVENTS

1. 0040hrs: Four MAS boats of the 18th MAS Division attack the minesweeper-destroyers led by Commander Kitcat. None of the four torpedo spreads hits any of the three destroyers, but in turning to avoid the torpedoes, two of them suffer damage to their minseweeping gear.

2. 0050hrs: At the other end of the convoy, four German S-Boats of the 3rd S-Boat Flotilla attack the rear of the convoy near Cape Bon, but again no ships are hit.

3. 0100hrs: Capitano di Corvetta Manuti commanding the 2nd MAS Boat Division spots a cruiser about 6–8km offshore. He has been waiting beside the wreck of the British destroyer *Havock*, which serves to hide him from both British lookouts and radar. He orders his six boats to race out and attack the *Manchester* and the merchant ships seen astern of her.

4. The British ships are illuminated by the beams from the lighthouses at Kelibia and Cape Bon, which greatly help the Axis crews locate the convoy.

5. 0102hrs: Four of the 2nd MAS Division boats pass ahead of *Manchester*, ready to attack the convoy from seaward.

6. Capitano Manuti in *MS-16* accompanied by *MS-22* attacks the light cruiser *Manchester* from her starboard beam. At 0104hrs and 0106hrs, the boats launch one torpedo each from ranges of 750–800m.

7. Captain Drew of *Manchester* fires at the approaching boats, and turns his ship to avoid the torpedoes. However, the cruiser is struck by one of the torpedoes on her starboard quarter. She quickly loses all power and stops dead in the water.

8. Astern of the *Manchester*, the *Almeria Lykes* followed by the *Glenorchy* both have to take evasive action to avoid colliding with the stricken warship.

9. On board the destroyer *Ashanti*, Rear Admiral Burrough learns of the damage to *Manchester*, and orders the destroyer *Pathfinder* to go on ahead to offer Drew whatever assistance he needs.

10. 0110hrs: *MS-26* of the 20th MAS Division attacks the *Rochester Castle*, and one of her torpedoes hits the merchant ship amidships on her port side. At the same moment, another MS boat crosses the bows of the *Dorset*, without launching any torpedoes.

The night battle, 13 August 1942

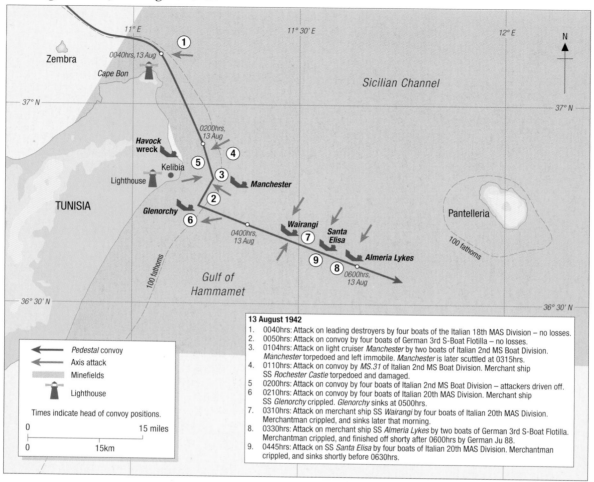

13 August 1942
1. 0040hrs: Attack on leading destroyers by four boats of the Italian 18th MAS Division – no losses.
2. 0050hrs: Attack on convoy by four boats of German 3rd S-Boat Flotilla – no losses.
3. 0104hrs: Attack on light cruiser *Manchester* by two boats of Italian 2nd MS Boat Division. *Manchester* torpedoed and left immobile. *Manchester* is later scuttled at 0315hrs.
4. 0110hrs: Attack on convoy by *MS.31* of Italian 2nd MS Boat Division. Merchant ship SS *Rochester Castle* torpedoed and damaged.
5. 0200hrs: Attack on convoy by four boats of Italian 2nd MS Boat Division – attackers driven off.
6. 0210hrs: Attack on convoy by four boats of Italian 20th MAS Division. Merchant ship SS *Glenorchy* crippled. *Glenorchy* sinks at 0500hrs.
7. 0310hrs: Attack on merchant ship SS *Wairangi* by four boats of Italian 20th MAS Division. Merchantman crippled, and sinks later that morning.
8. 0330hrs: Attack on merchant ship SS *Almeria Lykes* by two boats of German 3rd S-Boat Flotilla. Merchantman crippled, and finished off shorty after 0600hrs by German Ju 88.
9. 0445hrs: Attack on SS *Santa Elisa* by four boats of Italian 20th MAS Division. Merchantman crippled, and sinks shortly before 0630hrs.

At 0310hrs the fighting resumed at the head of the convoy. Two Italian MAS boats were spotted by *Kenya*. The cruiser opened fire, but it was clear she wasn't the target. The boats they were after were the two merchantmen in sight astern of the cruiser, the *Santa Elisa* and *Wairangi*. The attackers were from a new formation, the 20th MAS Division. The division commander Tenente Rolando Perasso in *MAS-552* and his consort Sottotenente Marco Calcagno in *MAS-554* had appeared to the north-east of *Kenya*, and both circled round her towards *Wairangi*, which lay off the cruiser's port quarter. Perasso launched his two torpedoes at just 200m, and was rewarded with one hit. The torpedo struck *Wairangi* amidships, beside No. 3 hold. The explosion ripped a hole in her port side, and while it didn't detonate the explosives stored there, the ship began flooding rapidly.

Wairangi was still afloat, but it was clear she was settling in the water. So, Captain Henry Gordon gave the order to abandon ship. After a couple of minutes, Perasso withdrew, pursued by shell splashes from *Kenya*'s salvoes. Calcagno in *MS-554* never pressed home his attack, though, and lingered out of range, waiting for another victim. The *Wairangi* managed to stay afloat, her decks awash and her half-submerged hulk ringed by her ship's boats. Just

before dawn two Ju 88s appeared and dropped two torpedoes apiece, but surprisingly these missed. Two hours later, just after 0800hrs, the destroyer *Somali* arrived and rescued all 79 survivors. Their merchantman eventually sank later that forenoon.

Next, it was the turn of the SS *Almeria Lykes*. A little after 0330hrs, she was sighted by the German S-boats *S-30* and *S-36*. They closed in on the American-flagged merchantman from astern. At the time, *Somali* was two miles ahead, with the minesweepers two miles further on. Nobody spotted the Germans, though, until they struck. Oberleutnant Horst Weber of *S-30* had been shadowing the *Almeria Lykes* for an hour. He finally made his move, racing towards the merchantman while Oberleutnant Brauns of *S-36* launched two torpedoes from 1,200m at *Somali*. They missed, but Weber launched his pair at the merchant ship from just 600m, and was rewarded by a hit. It struck the merchantman on her port side forward, beside No. 1 hold. The ship was fortunate – the sacks of flour stowed there absorbed much of the blast.

The hold flooded, though, and the *Almeria Lykes* lost power to her engines. Captain Henderson ordered his crew to abandon ship, and all 105 took to the ship's three boats while their attackers escaped into the darkness. Meanwhile, Sottotenente Calcagno in the Italian *MS-554* watched the German attack, and saw that their victim was still afloat. So, he closed in to launch his own two torpedoes. Although he later claimed to have sunk her, both of his torpedoes missed their target. Meanwhile, the *Almeria Lykes* boats clustered around their damaged ship. When it became clear the ship wasn't sinking, Henderson tried to persuade his crew to return on board to save her. All of them refused, save for Henderson, three officers and Lieutenant-Commander Mitchell, their British liaison officer. They set and fired the ship's scuttling charges, but these refused to detonate. So, the American crew remained where they were, until *Somali* and *Eskimo* appeared. Once his crew were rescued, Captain Henderson requested that *Somali*'s Commander Edmund Currey sink the American ship. Currey refused, as he intended to take her in tow. If the crew of *Almeria Lykes* had been more willing, their ship might well have been saved.

Meanwhile, another American merchantman was under attack. At 0445hrs, five miles to the north-west, the *Santa Elisa* was spotted by the rest of the 20th MAS Division. She was on her own, having become separated from the others earlier, and hoped to rejoin them before dawn. Instead she encountered *MAS-557*. The American ship's gunners had heard the Italian

An Italian Motoscafo Armato Silurante (MAS) boat, or 'torpedo-armed motor boat' in English. *MAS-563* was an MAS-555-type boat, and during *Pedestal* she formed part of the 15th MAS Division, which took part in the running night battle with the convoy south of Pantelleria.

Damaged and burning merchant ships from the *Pedestal* convoy, photographed from an Italian reconnaissance aircraft during the morning of 13 August. One of these was probably the SS *Almeria Lykes*, and the other the SS *Santa Elisa*, both of which were crippled and sunk.

engines and opened fire. After a brief exchange the MAS boat sheered away, spun round to launch a torpedo, then vanished again into the night. The torpedo missed, but another MAS boat then appeared on the *Santa Elisa*'s starboard beam. She was Tenente Giuseppe Iafrate's *MAS-564*, which closed to 300m before launching her own torpedoes. One of them struck the *Santa Elisa* on her starboard side forward, blowing a hole in No. 1 hold.

Unlike *Almeria Lykes*, though, she had aviation fuel stowed there, and this erupted in a fireball which sent a 500ft pillar of flame into the night sky. Within a minute, the fire was raging uncontrollably, and Captain T. Thompson ordered his men to take to the boats. All 28 of her crew survived, although some were badly injured, and they remained close by their blazing, half-submerged ship. The *Santa Elisa* finally sank just before dawn. At sunrise, her crew were rescued by the *Bramham* and *Penn*, which appeared from the west, escorting the SS *Port Chalmers*.

It had been a horrendous night for the *Pedestal* convoy. Burrough had been unable to regroup his convoy, and had paid the price. The *Glenorchy* had been sunk, and the *Almeria Lykes*, *Santa Elisa* and *Wairangi* crippled and unlikely to remain afloat. The *Ohio* and *Rochester Castle* were damaged, as was *Brisbane Star*, which had also become separated. Most of these damaged ships were now little more than sitting ducks. Burrough's hope was that RAF Malta Command could put enough fighters in the air to protect them. Burrough had also learned that six submarines from Malta's 10th Flotilla were nearby, to help protect the convoy against a surface attack by the Regia Marina. By then, though, Burrough had also learned that this very serious threat had dissipated during the night.

DA ZARA'S SORTIE

A major element in the Axis response to Operation *Pedestal* was the deployment of a powerful surface group of Italian warships. These were under the command of Ammiraglio da Zara, who during Operation *Harpoon* in June had come close to destroying the convoy off Pantelleria. Now, for *Pedestal* da Zara was to repeat his near success in the same waters. This time, though, he would have a larger force under his command. His own 7th Cruiser Division was made up of the light cruisers *Eugenio di Savoia* and *Raimondo Montecuccoli* based in Cagliari in Sardinia, supported by several destroyers. He would be reinforced by another light cruiser, the *Muzio Attendolo*, fresh from repair in Naples, and by the 3rd Cruiser Division, commanded by Ammiraglio Angelo Parona, which was based in Messina in Sicily and was made up of the heavy cruisers *Gorizia* and *Trieste*, and more destroyers. As the senior officer, da Zara was in overall command.

Da Zara's orders were to put to sea on the night of 11/12 August, and then take up a waiting position near the tiny island of Ustica in the Tyrrhenian Sea, north of Palermo and to the east of Cagliari. Parona would join him the following afternoon, as would the *Attendolo*. In previous convoy operations the convoy's powerful covering force would turn back to Gibraltar when it reached the Skerki Bank. If that happened again, da Zara's force would sail around the western side of Sicily, and intercept the convoy to the south of Pantelleria at dawn on 13 August. It was also to be allocated its own air cover of 45 Italian fighters.

Da Zara left Cagliari late in the evening of 11 August. Unluckily, this coincided with a raid on Sardinian airfields by RAF light bombers based in Malta, and one of them spotted the Italian force just before midnight, heading east. Air Vice Marshal Park used one of his radar-equipped Wellington bombers to attack the Italian cruisers in the early hours of 12 August. This was unsuccessful, but radar-equipped Wellingtons were then used to shadow da Zara's force throughout the following day. Shortly before noon on 12 August Parona sailed from Messina, and was joined by the *Attendolo*. Da Zara and Parona rendezvoused near Ustica at 1900hrs. They were also joined there by a third heavy cruiser, the *Trieste*, which had sailed from La Spezia. That gave da Zara three heavy cruisers, three light cruisers and 12 destroyers.

The Italian light cruiser *Raimondo Montecuccoli*, which formed part of Ammiraglio da Zara's 7th Cruiser Division during Operation *Pedestal*. She and her sister ship *Muzio Attendolo* and da Zara's flagship *Eugenio di Savoia*, a slightly enlarged version of the Montecuccoli class, all carried eight 6in. (15.2cm) guns, making them individually less powerful than their British counterparts.

The combined force then steamed towards the western coast of Sicily. Da Zara was aware that he was being shadowed due to the German FuMo 24 radar fitted in the destroyer *Legionario*. What he didn't know was that Park was also planning a dawn air strike on da Zara's force by 30 torpedo-armed Beauforts and Beaufighters, supported by Spitfires. This attack, though, never happened. That evening, Ammiraglio Arturo Riccardi, commander of the Supermarina, had second thoughts. During 12 August, he became concerned about the risks involved in a night action, particularly when he learned that Burrough had been reinforced by warships from Force Z.

This, combined with the risk of air and submarine attacks against da Zara's force, led to a loss of nerve. That evening, Riccardi contacted Mussolini, who, after conferring with Hitler, decided to abort the sortie. At 0051hrs, while 50km north-west of Sicily, da Zara was ordered to turn back. He would now take the 7th Cruiser Division to Naples, while Parona would lead the rest of the force back to Messina. It was an unfortunate decision for the Regia Marina. This unwittingly placed Parona's ships in the path of a patrolling British submarine. That evening, two British submarines from Malta were operating off the north coast of Sicily: *Safari* off Palermo, and *Unbroken* 130km to the east, near the Aeolian Islands, which lay near the approaches to the Strait of Messina.

By 0330hrs on 13 August, as the night battle for the convoy was resuming to the south of Pantelleria, *Unbroken* was patrolling off the island of Panarea, to the north-east of the main Aeolian archipelago. The boat's commander Lieutenant Alastair Mars had just been told that Parona was heading towards Messina, and felt that the island, near a deep-water channel through the archipelago, was a promising place to ambush him. Sure enough, at 0725hrs he spotted a line of ships approaching from the west: four cruisers in line astern, making 20 knots, with four destroyers deployed on either beam. *Attendolo* was in the lead, followed by *Bolzano*, *Gorizia* and *Trieste*. Two seaplanes patrolled overhead. Mars crept closer, and at 0800hrs he passed beneath the port destroyer screen. The cruisers were now just 3,000 yards ahead.

Mars noticed that the cruisers had slowed slightly, to allow *Gorizia* to launch her seaplane. At 0805hrs, he fired a spread of four torpedoes. Mars then turned away and dived to avoid the inevitable depth-charging.

Unbroken's torpedo tracks had been spotted, and the Italian cruisers tried to comb the tracks. *Bolzano*, though, didn't manage to do this, and 135 seconds after being fired, a 21in. Mark VIII torpedo struck her port quarter. The explosion ruptured an oil tank which ignited a major fire. Capitano Mario Mezzadra immediately flooded an adjacent magazine to save the ship. *Bolzano* was taking on water fast, though, so Mezzadra turned her towards Panarea and beached her there, to prevent her from sinking.

The second explosion was from the light cruiser *Muzio Attendolo*. The torpedo struck her bow, shearing it off as far as her A turret. However, Capitano Mario Schiavuta was able to seal off the damaged compartments, and so kept his cruiser afloat. That evening, she limped into Messina under her own power. *Unbroken* was then subjected to 45 minutes of depth-charging before she was able to creep away. By 18 August, she was back in Malta. *Bolzano* was refloated on 15 August and taken to Naples for repair. Like the *Attendolo*, though, she would take no further part in the war. It was a dramatic end to an operation which had held such promise for the Regia Marina. Essentially, though, a loss of nerve had spared the *Pedestal* convoy from what would almost certainly have been a death blow.

Progress of the *Pedestal* convoy, 13 August 1942

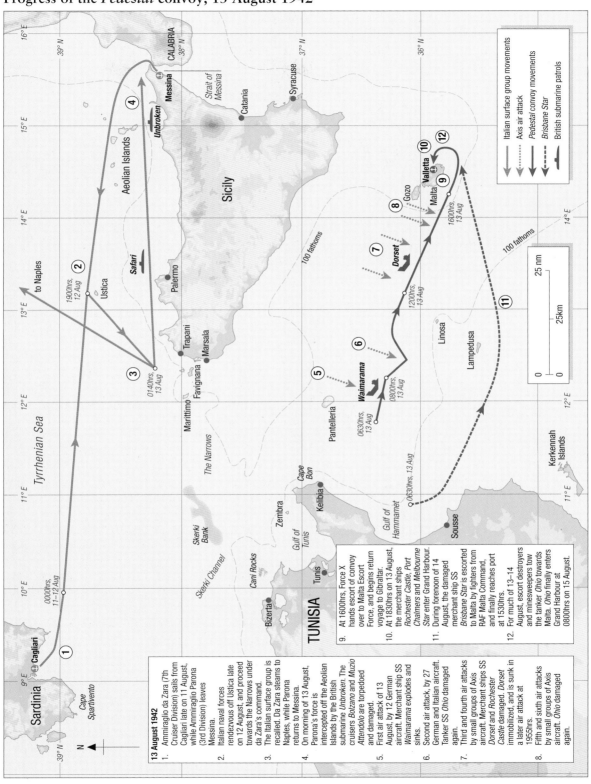

13 August 1942

1. Ammiraglio da Zara (7th Cruiser Division) sails from Cagliari late on 11 August, while Ammiraglio Parona (3rd Division) leaves Messina.

2. Italian naval forces rendezvous off Ustica late on 12 August, and proceed towards the Narrows under da Zara's command.

3. The Italian surface group is recalled. Da Zara steams to Naples, while Parona returns to Messina.

4. On morning of 13 August, Parona's force is intercepted off the Aeolian Islands by the British submarine *Unbroken*. The cruisers *Bolzano* and *Muzio Attendolo* are torpedoed and damaged.

5. First air attack of 13 August, by 12 German aircraft. Merchant ship SS *Waimarama* explodes and sinks.

6. Second air attack, by 27 German and Italian aircraft. Tanker SS *Ohio* damaged again.

7. Third and fourth air attacks by small groups of Axis aircraft. Merchant ships SS *Dorset* and *Rochester Castle* damaged. *Dorset* immobilized, and is sunk in a later air attack at 1955hrs.

8. Fifth and sixth air attacks by small groups of Axis aircraft. *Ohio* damaged again.

9. At 1600hrs, Force X hands escort of convoy over to Malta Escort Force, and begins return voyage to Gibraltar.

10. At 1830hrs on 13 August, the merchant ships *Rochester Castle*, *Port Chalmers* and *Melbourne Star* enter Grand Harbour. During forenoon of 14 August, the damaged merchant ship SS *Brisbane Star* is escorted to Malta by fighters from RAF Malta Command, and finally reaches port at 1530hrs.

11. For much of 13–14 August, escort destroyers and minesweepers tow the tanker *Ohio* towards Malta. *Ohio* finally enters Grand Harbour at 0800hrs on 15 August.

77

THE LAST AIR ATTACKS, 13 AUGUST

On the morning of 13 August, the sun rose at 0634hrs. The day was clear and bright, with only scattered clouds. It was perfect flying weather. At 0710hrs, the *Dorset*, to the north-west of the main body of the convoy, saw 12 Ju 88s pass overhead, heading towards the south-west. To Captain Tuckett, it looked like they intended to attack the crippled merchantmen astern of them. Lieutenant Baines in *Bramham* saw them, too, as he headed towards the *Santa Elisa*, with orders to sink the cargo ship with gunfire. Then, at 0715hrs, he watched a lone Ju 88 attack the American vessel, scoring three direct hits. The *Santa Elisa* sank within five minutes. Baines then turned away to rejoin the convoy, and on reaching the *Dorset*, he took station off her port side, as she rejoined the convoy.

This initial attack on the crippled ships gave Burrough in *Ashanti* the breathing space he needed to regroup the convoy. At dawn, the *Ashanti* had come upon the *Melbourne Star*, which was redirected towards the other merchant ships. At 0730hrs, Burrough detached *Somali* and *Eskimo* to search for *Manchester*, and to rescue any survivors from the cruiser or the crippled merchantmen. They duly picked up men from the *Almeria Lykes* and the *Wairangi* as they sped west towards Kelibia. At 1040hrs, they came upon the site where *Manchester* sank, and rescued 150 survivors from the water. They could see several hundred more on the shore, marching inland guarded by Vichy French troops.

To the south-east of Pantelleria, after the departure of the two destroyers, Burrough's Force Z was now made up of nine warships. These were the cruisers *Charybdis* and *Kenya* (the latter with her bow blown off), five destroyers (his own temporary flagship *Ashanti*, as well as *Fury*, *Icarus*, *Intrepid* and *Pathfinder*) and the escort destroyers *Bramham* and *Penn*. He had also gathered together five merchant ships: *Dorset*, *Melbourne Star*, *Port Chalmers*, *Rochester Castle* and *Waimarama*. Several miles to the west, the damaged tanker *Ohio*, accompanied by the escort destroyer *Ledbury*, were coming up astern, making 16 knots. So, despite the horrors of the night, the *Pedestal* convoy was finally being gathered together into a reasonably

Early on 13 August, the elegant passenger liner SS *Waimarama* was bombed by a flight of Ju 88s, and she was torn apart when a bomb exploded, detonating her cargo of munitions and fuel. Here the smoking pyre of the merchantman is pictured from the SS *Dorset*.

defensible formation. It was just as well. At 0800hrs, a second wave of 12 Ju 88s from KG 54 and KG 77 appeared from the north.

At that moment, the *Charybdis* was leading a column of three merchantmen: *Rochester Castle*, then *Waimarama*, with *Melbourne Star* at the rear. Escorts were ranged on each beam, while *Kenya* and *Ashanti* were close by, screening the *Port Chalmers*. Two miles off their port quarter were *Dorset* and *Bramham*, while five miles astern was *Ohio* and *Ledbury*. So, Burrough's concentration was still under way when the German bombers struck. The attack was led by three Ju 88s, one behind the other. They approached the convoy from astern, and despite a heavy barrage and the weaving of the convoy, the first of them managed to drop its bombs over the *Waimarama*. The graceful passenger-liner was struck by four bombs. They landed abaft her funnel, and their detonation set off the ammunition and aviation fuel stored in her after holds. The *Waimarama* was ripped apart: a bridge lookout peered aft and saw the rest of the ship had disappeared.

A column of smoke and flame shot hundreds of feet into the air, engulfing the second Junkers, which was destroyed. Burning fuel oil spilled over the sea, igniting the water around the ship. *Waimarama*'s bow rose up as the crushed remnants of the stern broke away, and her hull filled with water. She sank in less than two minutes. Astern of her the *Melbourne Star* was showered with flaming debris. Captain David MacFarlane had to turn hard to port to avoid colliding with the sinking ship. The third Ju 88 dropped her bombs over the *Melbourne Star*, but thanks to the turn these all missed her.

This manoeuvre, though, placed the *Melbourne Star* squarely amid the burning oil. Small fires erupted on her decks, and flames seared the ship's side. This proved too much for the crew of her after guns, who jumped overboard into a patch of open water. The *Melbourne Star*, though, passed through the burning sea without her cargo igniting. The survivors of the *Waimarama* who had jumped into the water then saw the bows of *Ledbury* appear through the flames. Despite orders from Burrough to keep clear, Lieutenant-Commander Roger Hill conned his small warship into the inferno, and lowered a boat to pluck the survivors to safety. At one point, though, Hill backed out of the flames to fire at the next wave of German bombers, before returning to complete the rescue. In the end, 18 survivors from *Waimarama* were saved, together with the 33 from *Melbourne Star* who had abandoned ship. Another 87 from *Waimarama* were lost, while one of those rescued later died of his injuries.

At the time *Waimarama* had been hit, *Ledbury* had been coming up astern with the *Ohio*. As his escort surged ahead, Captain Mason steered the *Ohio* around the patch of burning sea. Meanwhile, the air attacks were still under way. Four torpedo-armed Ju 88s from I./KG 54 attacked the *Rochester Castle* just as the merchantman astern of her exploded. Her decks were showered with burning debris, too, but the torpedoes passed her by. The rest of the air attack proved unsuccessful, as the remaining bombers sheered away from the *Waimarama*'s funeral pyre, and from the barrage thrown up by Burrough's escorts. The convoy had suffered a grievous loss during this first major air attack of the day, but at least the remaining merchantmen were largely unscathed. Burrough, though, fully expected more attacks that morning.

A Ju 87 Stuka dive-bomber releasing a 250kg bomb. Once committed to a dive, the Stuka pilot had to drop his bomb and then pull out before the aircraft approached within 300m of his target. An alarm sounded in the cockpit once the aircraft descended past 500m.

By now, the first long-range British Beaufighters had appeared from Malta, a hundred miles to the east. This in itself was frustrating, as without *Nigeria* and *Cairo* Burrough lacked any form of fighter control, and he was unable to communicate with the airmen. Still, it was a promise of better protection to come. After the bombers flew off, Burrough reorganized his battered convoy. It was re-formed into two columns, with *Kenya* leading the port one (made up of *Rochester Castle* and then *Dorset*) and a starboard column led by *Charybdis* (followed by *Melbourne Star*, *Ohio* and *Port Chalmers*). The smaller escorts were deployed in line astern on each beam of the convoy.

The next air attack began at 0925hrs. This time, 15 Ju 87s of I./StG 3 were preceded by 12 SM.79 and SM.84 torpedo-bombers from 132° Gruppo, carrying Motobombas. These were dropped five miles ahead of the convoy, but as had happened before, Burrough altered course, and the aerial mines were avoided. The Italian bombers and their covering fighters withdrew, but the Stukas were more persistent. This time they targeted the *Ohio*. Burrough had *Ashanti* leave the starboard escort column and ranged close alongside the tanker, to give her as much close-range AA protection as he could. A near miss from a 250kg bomb off *Ohio*'s port bow caused minor flooding forward, but more serious was the diving Stuka brought down by *Ashanti*, which crashed onto the tanker's poop deck. Fortunately for the *Ohio*, it had already released its bomb, and although the tanker's after gun was wrecked, no significant damage was done.

As the air attack developed, Beaufighters engaged the departing bombers, followed by long-range Spitfires. One Spitfire shot down an SM.84, but another British fighter fell foul of the over-zealous gunners of *Dorset*, and was shot down. The next attack came 15 minutes later, at 0940hrs. It was made by nine Ju 88s, and targeted *Kenya*. Captain Russell deftly avoided the bombs, although near misses showered the cruiser's decks with bomb fragments. Then, at 0955hrs, *Charybdis* detected two new waves of aircraft on her radar. In a well-orchestrated attack, 20 Ju 88s from KG 77 attacked the convoy from the east, while 18 Ju 87s from I./StG 3 approached it from the west. By now, there were more British fighters above the convoy, and these engaged the bombers and their accompanying fighters first. Then it was the turn of the convoy escorts.

One Ju 88 was hit as it released its bomb-load, and it spiralled down into the sea, only to strike the starboard bow of the *Ohio*. Fortunately, there was no explosion, though aircraft wreckage was strewn across the tanker's

A bomb lands close to SS *Dorset*, during an air attack on the morning of 13 August. Near misses like this could buckle hull plates, causing flooding, and if the bomb detonated on hitting the water, it could pepper the ship's superstructure with bomb fragments. The photograph was taken from one of the Force X escorts.

forecastle. However, other near misses caused more of the tanker's hull plates to buckle, and flooding knocked out her boilers in a spray of steam. The *Ohio* was now immobile. Burrough immediately ordered *Bramham*, *Ledbury* and *Penn* to form a defensive cordon around her. Similarly, another near miss caused similar damage to *Dorset*, reducing her to just one engine, and a top speed of 11 knots. *Rochester Castle* also suffered from near misses, which buckled her hull and flooded her machinery spaces. Fortunately, her engineers got the ship moving again at 1025hrs. The Germans then withdrew, pursued by the Spitfires.

Ohio was now dropping astern of the convoy. After a 75-minute lull, the enemy aircraft returned at 1120hrs. This time the assailants were 12

The SS *Rochester Castle* entering Grand Harbour, Malta in the early evening of 13 August. She had been hit amidships by a torpedo, but the damage was contained – although here she can be seen sitting low in the water.

The SS *Port Chalmers*, which also entered Grand Harbour on 13 August, was relatively unscathed, save for some light damage from near misses or falling debris. She was the flagship of the Convoy Commodore.

SM.79 torpedo-bombers from 130° Gruppo, transferred to Sicily from Sardinia that morning, escorted by 14 fighters. They attacked from the south this time, catching the patrolling Spitfires off guard. Seeing this, and defying orders, Commander Gibbs pulled *Pathfinder* out of the starboard convoy screen, and making 30 knots he turned towards the approaching bombers. *Pathfinder*, with all guns blazing, was targeted by several torpedoes, but Gibbs avoided them. His distraction had probably prevented serious damage to the convoy. *Pathfinder* even managed to down a torpedo-bomber. After a few minutes, the bombers withdrew, chased by the Spitfires. However, not all of the Italian torpedoes had been aimed at *Pathfinder*. One almost hit the *Port Chalmers*, the pennant ship of Commodore Venables. She was still streaming her own minesweeping paravanes, and the torpedo became lodged in her starboard sweep gear. She stopped while the gear was ditched, and then got under way again without suffering any damage.

It was now almost noon. It was becoming clear that the convoy was becoming increasingly better protected by the Spitfires of RAF Malta Command. So, Burrough detached *Ledbury*, sending her back to look for survivors. He also ordered *Bramham* and *Penn* to continue to escort the lagging *Ohio* and *Dorset*. That allowed the rest of Force Z to press on to Malta with the three largely undamaged merchantmen. After all, they were now nearing the entrance to the swept channel through the minefield that surrounded the island. There, he had arranged to meet mineweepers from the Malta Escort Force, which would lead the *Melbourne Star*, *Port Chalmers* and *Rochester Castle* into Valletta's Grand Harbour. As they drew closer, making a steady 16 knots, Spitfires flew cover overhead, an extremely reassuring sight.

Finally, at 1530hrs, as they reached the swept channel, they were met by Commander Henry Jerome with the minesweepers *Speedy*, *Hebe*, *Hythe* and *Rye*. Burrough duly handed over his three charges, then turned away

again to the east. Their job done, the two cruisers and four destroyers of Force X could now return to Gibraltar. Just over two hours later, at 1800hrs, they passed *Ohio*, accompanied by *Penn*, while yet more Spitfires flew protective cover overhead. As he passed, Burrough in *Ashanti* flashed a signal to Captain Mason of *Ohio*. It read: 'I am proud to have known you.' Meanwhile, Jerome's minesweepers were untroubled by enemy aircraft as they led the three merchant ships through the channel which rounded Malta's eastern side, before reaching Valletta and Grand Harbour. Finally, at 1830hrs, *Rochester Castle*, followed by *Port Chalmers* and then *Melbourne Star* limped into the harbour, watched by thousands of cheering onlookers lining the shore. This was an emotional moment, as it marked the temporary relief of Malta, and allowed it to remain defiant, until more supplies could reach the beleaguered island. This, though, wasn't the end of the story. Two more merchant ships and a tanker were still at sea, desperately trying to reach the same haven.

The SS *Melbourne Star* of the Blue Star Line entering Grand Harbour on 13 August. Some of her crew had jumped overboard that morning, fearing their ship was about to explode, but the merchantman made it through to Malta with only superficial fire damage to show for her experience.

THE STRAGGLERS

As darkness fell on 13 August, Force X retraced its old course, heading west towards the Tunisian coast. Burrough, still flying his flag in *Ashanti*, was accompanied by *Charybdis* and *Kenya*, and the destroyers *Fury*, *Icarus*, *Intrepid* and *Pathfinder*. Their speed was limited by *Kenya*, but even with her damaged bow the cruiser could still make 20 knots. That meant Burrough expected to reach Cape Bon at around 0100hrs the following morning. Sure

The bows of the light cruiser *Kenya*, pictured in dry dock after being struck by a torpedo on 12 August. Despite this dramatic damage, her forepeak was sealed off to prevent further flooding, and she was able to make 20 knots, and so could keep up with the convoy.

enough, they passed the headland at 0130hrs, where a half-hearted attack by two MAS boats was driven off by *Kenya*'s guns. They continued west, and after crossing the Bay of Tunis, they hugged the coast. The next alarm came at 0450hrs, when they were passing the Fratelli Islands. The Italian submarine *Granito* spotted them while on the surface, and Tenente Leo Sposito fired a spread of four torpedoes. These passed between *Ashanti* and *Kenya*, and Captain Russell reacted by trying to ram the submarine with his cruiser. It was probably fortunate he didn't succeed. When *Granito* dived to escape, rather than hunt her, Burrough ordered his ships to leave her be, and sped off to the west.

An hour later, they were south of the Galite Islands, having left the coast to steam due west. The night before, just to the north of the island, another drama had unfolded. That was where the destroyer *Foresight* had been crippled late on 12 August. Throughout the night, Commander Tyrwhitt of *Tartar* had tried to tow the *Foresight* to safety. These attempts were unsuccessful, and at 0830hrs on 13 August, *U-73* spotted them, and Kapitänleutnant Rosenbaum fired a spread of torpedoes at the destroyers. They missed, and *U-73* was driven off by *Tartar*'s depth charges. By then, though, it was clear that *Foresight* was doomed. So, at 0955hrs, after her crew were taken off, *Foresight* was scuttled by one of *Tartar*'s torpedoes. *Tartar* then returned to Gibraltar. Two other destroyers crowded with survivors, *Eskimo* and *Somali*, also reached Gibraltar safely at 0530hrs on 15 August. Having driven off a last series of air attacks on 14 August, Burrough's Force X finally reached Gibraltar at 1800hrs the following evening.

Meanwhile, the final stages of the *Pedestal* drama were being played out to the west of Malta. On the evening of 12 August, the *Brisbane Star* had her bow wrecked by an aerial torpedo, and was unable to keep up with the convoy. So, Captain Riley decided to head inshore, and try to get through to Malta on his own. *Brisbane Star* rounded Cape Bon behind the convoy, making 5 knots, then continued south into the Gulf of Hammamet. Soon after dawn, though, off the Tunisian port of Sousse, they were intercepted by a Vichy French patrol boat. When its commander ordered Riley to put in to Sousse, he pleaded his case, stressing that his cargo included relief supplies for Malta. The French officer relented, and allowed Riley to continue his journey.

They then headed directly towards Malta, but unrest among the crew was simmering, as the threat of enemy attacks increased. Still, the ship continued on its way, untroubled by the enemy until the following morning. At dawn on 14 August, though, they were spotted by a lone Ju 88, which swooped down to attack them. Its bombs missed, and the merchantman's gunners hit their assailant, which limped off, chased by a freshly arrived flight of Beaufighters. Shortly afterwards, Spitfires arrived from Malta to protect them. The rest of the day proved uneventful, and the *Brisbane Star*, now making 10 knots, finally entered Malta's Grand Harbour at 1530hrs that afternoon. That made her the fourth ship of the convoy to make it into port.

Meanwhile that morning, as the *Brisbane Star* was still 50 miles south of Pantelleria, the crew of the *Dorset* were trying to repair their ship. She already had an engine disabled, the result of a near miss the previous evening. Another close call at 1004hrs that morning caused more flooding, which put her remaining engine out of action. So, *Dorset* fell behind the convoy. Fortunately, though, Burrough sent Lieutenant Baines in *Bramham* to protect the ship as her crew tried to get her moving again. These near misses had also started a fire in her after hold. Without power to work the pumps, effective firefighting was impossible. So, at 1100hrs, Captain Tuckett decided he had to abandon ship. At that moment, though, *Bramham* arrived, and Baines offered to take the *Dorset* under tow.

This towing attempt was aborted shortly before noon, as *Bramham* fought off another bombing attack by two Ju 88s. Meanwhile, *Dorset* settled further, until shortly after 1300hrs, Baines agreed that she had to be scuttled. When he radioed for permission, Vice Admiral Ralph Leatham in Malta refused to countenance it. Baines' senior, Lieutenant-Commander James Swain of *Penn*, then ordered him to temporarily leave *Dorset*, and help him save the *Ohio*, a few miles away to the south-east. So, *Dorset* was abandoned, as Tuckett and his crew transferred to the *Bramham*. When the mineweeper *Rye* arrived to help the *Ohio*, *Bramham* returned to the *Dorset*, arriving just in time to fend off an attack by five Ju 88s.

Tuckett and some of his crew then reboarded *Dorset*, but the heat was now intense, as the fire was raging uncontrollably, and she was settling fast. At 1902hrs, the problem was taken out of the hands of Baines and Tuckett: four Ju 88s appeared from the north and bombed *Dorset*, damaging her further. There was now nothing Tuckett could do, so he and his men were brought to safety, and at 1925hrs *Dorset* began to sink. *Bramham* remained close by until the merchantman finally disappeared 30 minutes later. Baines then set off to rejoin the *Ohio*, his decks crowded with *Dorset*'s survivors.

The Blue Star Line's SS *Brisbane Star* finally reached Malta in the afternoon of 14 August. Her bow had been punctured by an aerial torpedo, and having become detached from the convoy, she continued on to Malta independently.

On the way, they were subjected to another air attack by a mixed force of 20 Ju 88s and Ju 87s. Baines, though, skilfully dodged the bombs, and rejoined *Penn* and *Ohio* at 2030hrs that evening.

The saga of the battered *Ohio* is one of the most famous events of the whole *Pedestal* story. The air attacks of earlier that morning had left her immobilized, with the wreckage of enemy aircraft littering her decks. Her electrical pumps had stopped working, and all that remained was her emergency steering system, which meant her rudder could still operate. As the rest of the convoy hauled away towards Malta, Burrough detached Lieutenant-Commander Swain in *Penn*, with orders to protect the tanker, and help her get under way. Attempts were made to rig a towline, but this was abandoned when the hawser parted at 1430hrs. By then it was found that ripped-open hull plates below the tanker's waterline were providing enough resitance to make the towing attempt untenable. Swain needed more power. He recalled *Bramham* to help, while word came from Malta that the minesweeper *Rye* was on its way to assist, accompanied by two motor launches.

Meanwhile, the crew of the *Ohio* were transferred to the *Penn*, as the immobile tanker was now little more than a floating target for Axis aircraft and submarines. The *Rye* arrived at 1820hrs, allowing *Bramham* to return to help *Dorset*. Captain Mason and his crew duly returned aboard the *Ohio*, and the towing attempt was resumed. It was soon found, though, that *Penn* and *Rye* lacked the power to move the tanker at anything faster than a slow walking pace. Then, at 1900hrs, just as darkness was falling, eight Ju 88s appeared. The towing hawser was slipped as *Penn* manoeuvred to fight off the attack. *Ohio* was hit by a 250kg bomb that struck her boat deck, killing a gun crew and damaging the engine room below. Worse, another near miss wrecked the tanker's rudder.

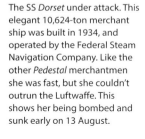

The SS *Dorset* under attack. This elegant 10,624-ton merchant ship was built in 1934, and operated by the Federal Steam Navigation Company. Like the other *Pedestal* merchantmen she was fast, but she couldn't outrun the Luftwaffe. This shows her being bombed and sunk early on 13 August.

Once again, the remaining crew of the *Ohio* transferred to the *Penn*, as the *Ohio*, now riding low in the water, was likely to founder. Swain also lost one motor launch, *ML-168*, which had been damaged by a near miss, and sent back to Malta. A little later *Bramham* rejoined them, and when it became clear the *Ohio* wasn't about to sink, Swain decided to make another attempt at towing the rudderless ship. This time, to avoid her skewing off course, *Rye* would tow from ahead, while *Penn* kept her in line using a

line astern. Meanwhile, *Bramham* and the remaining motor launch *ML-121* would protect them from predatory night-fighters or submarines. The tow began at 2350hrs, but *Rye* made almost no headway.

After 90 minutes, Baines brought *Bramham* alongside *Penn*, and suggested they use both escort destroyers – one on each beam of the tanker. So, they tried again, and this time there was an immediate improvement – they began moving forward at just over 6 knots. Then, at 0230hrs, *Rye*'s towing hawser parted. Realizing everyone was exhausted, Swain decided to wait until dawn before resuming the attempt.

Sunrise on 14 August revealed calm seas and clear skies. With it came the renewed threat of air attack. It also brought reinforcements, as at 0630hrs, *Ledbury* was spotted approaching from the west. She was carrying survivors from *Waimarama* and *Melbourne Star*, and many of these volunteered to help. So, Lieutenant Hill transferred them onto *Ohio* to man her undamaged AA guns, and clear her decks of wreckage.

Even more importantly, helped by *Waimarama*'s experienced boatswain, Captain Mason was able to return on board with some of his crew, and help re-rig the towing hawsers, while engineers from *Penn* went on board the tanker with a compressor to pump out some of the water from her machinery spaces. Mason noted that the tanker's back now appeared to be broken, and she was riding very low in the water. She was still afloat, though, and now, with *Ledbury* joining in tandem with *Rye*, the towing resumed. Although the hawser parted again, this was replaced, and the tow restarted. At 1030hrs, the minesweeper *Speedy* arrived carrying Lieutenant-Commander Jerome of the Malta Escort Force, who took charge of the operation. Progress was still slow, and at 1102hrs the tow had to be slipped again as nine Italian Stukas were seen approaching from the north. This time the tanker was able to defend herself, and her gunners even managed to shoot down one of the attackers. The others were chased off by a squadron of Spitfires which suddenly appeared overhead, and another Stuka was shot down as it tried to escape.

The respite this brought was brief. At 1114hrs, another wave of eight Stukas appeared, just as the reattached towing hawser parted again. This time, *Bramham* hauled off to port to help break up the wave of bombers as they commenced their dive. All of the 250kg bombs missed the *Ohio*, although some of these caused yet more damage to her broken hull. One, exploding just off her stern, wrecked her stern transom – but *Ohio* still survived. The towing resumed once the Stukas withdrew, with *Bramham* on

The Hunt-class escort destroyer *Bramham* was one of several warships of her type to form part of the *Pedestal* convoy's escort. Together with her sister ship *Penn*, *Bramham* nursed the crippled tanker *Ohio* into Malta, in a stunning demonstration of perseverance and seamanship.

The damaged tanker SS *Ohio*, pictured from the escort destroyer *Ledbury* as she tries to pass a towing hawser to the badly damaged ship. The extensive efforts to save the tanker and bring her into port finally paid off.

Ohio's port side, *Penn* to starboard, and *Rye* towing from ahead. Soon they were making a steady 6 knots. To cheer everyone up, Swain repeatedly played a record of *Chattanooga Choo Choo* through his ship's tannoy. *Ledbury* and *Speedy* provided the AA escort, while Spitfires flew overhead. Finally, just before sunset, the coast of Malta was sighted ahead.

A civilian tug came out from Malta to help, but only managed to collide with *Penn*. Jerome ordered the lubberly tug back to Valletta. They finally reached the mouth of the swept channel at 0200hrs on 15 August. There, *Rye* dropped the tow, as it was clear *Bramham* and *Penn* were able to keep the tanker moving on their own. Instead, *Rye* and *Speedy* went on ahead, checking the channel for rogue mines. The channel had two bends, though, and *Ledbury* was used as a makeshift tug, to help turn the tanker onto her new course. At sunrise, the Harbour Master and Chief Pilot arrived, bringing three tugs with them to guide the tanker in. Finally, at 0800hrs on the day the Maltese called the Feast of Santa Marija, the *Ohio* finally entered Grand Harbour, cheered on by brass bands and thousands of islanders. As Lieutenant Hill of *Ledbury* recalled later: 'It was the most wonderful moment of my life'.

Within hours, the *Ohio*'s precious fuel was being offloaded, with the same speed as the island's stevedores had unloaded the equally vital cargo of the four *Pedestal* merchant ships which had preceded her into port. Operation *Pedestal* had finally come to a successful end. The losses had been extremely high, but these five ships had achieved the convoy's objective. Now, with sufficient food, ammunition, spares and fuel, Malta's garrison and civilian population could survive, and continue to resist the enemy. Congratulatory messages were flying everywhere, and cheering crowds wanted to thank the grimy and exhausted crewmen who had achieved the 'Miracle of Santa Marija'. For the men themselves, though, after their injured shipmates had been taken to hospital, and the survivors from other ships led ashore to be cared for, all most of them wanted to do was to sleep. After the most gruelling few days of their lives, they most heartily deserved it.

AFTERMATH

It was fortunate that the Axis made no air attack on Grand Harbour as the *Pedestal* ships were unloading. Instead, Operation *Ceres* worked smoothly. This was the mobilizing of the port's workforce, supported by servicemen, to rapidly unload the cargo, or pump fuel though pre-laid hoses into storage tanks. In all, some 32,000 tons of supplies had been delivered to Malta – enough to keep the island going for at least two more months. The fuel from *Ohio* also allowed RAF Malta Command's fighters to remain flying – a necessity if the island was to defend itself against further bomber raids. While more fuel and general supplies would have been welcome, given the hardships suffered by the *Pedestal* convoy it was something of a miracle that these five ships had actually made it into port. The Maltese as well as the island's garrison were still on extremely short rations, but it meant that the threat of widespread starvation had abated. It would be mid-November 1942 before the siege of Malta was finally lifted, following the arrival of a relief convoy from Port Said. By January 1943, a regular flow of convoys had been established through the Eastern Mediterranean. None of this would have been possible without *Pedestal*.

The crippled tanker *Ohio* entering Grand Harbour on the morning of 15 August, flanked by two escort destroyers, *Bramham* to port and *Penn* to starboard. It was their engines that carried the tanker into Malta, and helped keep her afloat long enough to reach port.

What *Pedestal* did, too, was to resurrect the threat Malta posed to Axis supply lines. Now, with both the RAF bombers and the submarines of the 10th Flotilla given the fuel they needed, attacks on enemy sea routes could be resumed. Rommel was therefore denied much of the supplies he needed to keep his DAK fully supplied, at a time when British supplies brought to Egypt around Africa ensured that Eighth Army was fully combat-ready. This as much as anything else played a part in Rommel's subsequent reverses at Alam Halfa and El Alamein. The Allied landings in French North Africa also played a part, as by the end of 1942 it led to the extension of Allied control along the North African coast from Morocco to Tunisia. This was followed in 1943 by the surrender of the last Axis forces in North Africa, and then the Allied invasion of Sicily, bringing with it the opening up of the Narrows to Allied shipping. Malta had now been returned to its pre-war status as the naval hub of the Mediterranean.

Thanks to *Pedestal*, the island which most had deemed indefensible in 1940 had managed to hold out against the most sustained bombing campaign of the war in the Mediterranean. The cost, though, had been high – some 1,600 Maltese civilians had been killed in the siege, together with 600 servicemen. The Royal Navy had lost dozens of ships during the Malta convoy operations, as had the merchant service, while over 4,000 sailors of both services had lost their lives. Ultimately, though, this cost – however high – had been worth paying, as the retention of Malta proved the deciding

The SS *Ohio* finally reached Malta on the morning of 15 August, having been nursed there by the escort destroyers *Bramham* and *Penn*. Here, *Bramham* still lies off her port side, but *Penn* has cast off, to allow tugs to lead the tanker into harbour.

factor in the War in the Mediterranean. The fortress island described as a thorn in the Axis side had been more than that. It had served as a symbol of defiance which had been pivotal in the fight against the Axis powers. If Malta had fallen, then the history of the war might have taken a very different course. Thanks to the officers and men of the *Pedestal* convoy and its escorts, this small beacon of democracy had managed to stay alight during these challenging and world-changing events.

Afterwards, Churchill wrote of Operation *Pedestal*: 'The reward justified the price exacted. Revictualled and resupplied with ammunition and vital stores, the strength of Malta revived. Submarines returned to the island, and with the striking forces of the Royal Air Force regained their dominating position in the Central Mediterranean'. This wasn't strictly true: the 10th Flotilla had been operating from Grand Harbour before *Pedestal*. What was certain, though, was that without *Ohio*'s fuel, these submarines and aircraft would almost certainly have been withdrawn from the island. The success of Operation *Pedestal* was more accurately measured in the island's survival, and its continued resistance.

A more accurate assesment was provided by Syfret himself: 'The losses suffered ... were regrettably heavy, and the number of merchant ships which reached Malta were disappointingly small ... The task of Force X was always difficult and hazardous. Nevertheless they continued undaunted and determined, and fighting their way through the many and heavy attacks by U-boats and E-boats and aircraft, they delivered five of their charges to Malta, and fought their way back to Gibraltar.' Syfret then praised the courage and determination of the officers and men of the merchant ships. He concluded: 'Many of these fine men and their ships were lost but the memory of their conduct will remain an inspiration to all who were privileged to sail with them'. It would be difficult to find a more fitting tribute to the sailors of Operation *Pedestal*, whichever service they came from.

THE LEGACY OF *PEDESTAL*

No memorials could be erected where these ferocious battles took place. The passage of Operation *Pedestal* from Gibraltar to Malta is only marked by a trail of once-proud ships on the seabed. *Eagle, Foresight, Cairo, Empire Hope, Deucalion, Clan Ferguson, Manchester, Glenorchy, Wairangi, Almeria Lykes, Santa Elisa, Waimarama* and *Dorset* still remain where they sank, their corroding hulls now havens for marine life. So, too, do the remains of some of their opponents, the submarines *Bronzo* and *Cobalto*. Some of these sites have been located and recorded – *Manchester*, for instance, has been extensively photographed underwater, as has *Eagle*. The seabed of the Mediterranean, though, is also littered with a trail of wrecked aircraft, both Allied and Axis, and by the remnants of expended ordnance. Even the ships which survived are no longer with us, having been taken to the breaker's yard long ago. They remain only in photographs and paintings, in stirring clips of film and in ship models.

Fortunately, we are well served in surviving accounts of the convoy, and by the written or spoken and recorded memories of those sailors and airmen

The entrance to Malta's National War Museum, Fort St Elmo. (HH58, CC BY-SA 4.0)

who took part in *Pedestal*. In terms of museum collections, the most extensive is that of the Malta National War Museum in Valletta, which has over 12,000 photographs in its archives, together with artefacts which directly relate to the *Pedestal* battles. These include the Union flag flown by the *Ohio* during the operation, together with her ship's wheel and nameplate, the latter recovered from a Maltese scrapyard. The one remaining wartime British cruiser, HMS *Belfast*, lies in the Pool of London, maintained as a historic vessel by the Imperial War Museum. She is similar to *Manchester*, *Kenya* and *Nigeria*, all of which featured prominently in the *Pedestal* story, and a visit aboard her tells us more about life in these ships than any photograph collection ever could.

Both the Imperial War Museum in London and the National Maritime Museum in nearby Greenwich have relevant collections and displays, albeit none which directly touches on *Pedestal*. So, too, does the Royal Naval Museum in Portsmouth, and the Museum of Naval Firepower in nearby Gosport. The Fleet Air Arm Museum in Yeovilton includes several of the aircraft which took part in *Pedestal*, as does the Royal Air Force Museum in Hendon. The Italian Air Force Museum at Lake Bracciano outside Rome is well worth a visit, as is the Military Historic Museum at Berlin-Gatow Airport and the Naval Technical Museum in La Spezia. There is a surviving U-boat in the Chicago Museum of Science and Industry, along with a Ju 87 Stuka, while another U-boat is housed at the Laboe Naval Memorial near Kiel. None of these, though, can truly conjure up the sensation of manning an AA gun while utterly exhausted, and watching the bombs falling towards you from an enemy dive-bomber. Virtually all of those who survived this experience are no longer among us. However, they, and the story of the momentous events they took part in, will be remembered.

The Grand Harbour, Valletta, photographed in 2010. (ianpudsey, CC BY 3.0)

FURTHER READING

Bragadin, Marc'Antonio, *The Italian Navy in World War II*, United States Naval Institute, Annapolis MD, 1957

Brescia, Maurizio, *Mussolini's Navy: A Reference Guide to the Regia Marina 1930–45*, Seaforth Publishing, Barnsley, 2012

Campbell, John, *Naval Weapons of World War Two*, Conway Maritime Press, London, 1985

Freidman, Norman, *Naval Radar*, Harper Collins, London, 1981

Gardiner, Robert (ed.), *Conway's All the World's Fighting Ships, 1922–1946*, Conway Maritime Press, London, 1980

Gardiner, Robert (ed.); *The Eclipse of the Big Gun: The Warship, 1906–45* (History of the Ship series), Conway Maritime Press, London, 1992

Greene, Jack and Massignani, Alessandro, *The Naval War in the Mediterranean 1940–43*, Chatham Publishing, Rochester, 1998

Hastings, Max, *Operation Pedestal: The Fleet that Battled to Malta 1942*, William Collins, London, 2021

Heathcote, Tony, *The British Admirals of the Fleet 1734–1995*, Pen & Sword, Barnsley, 2002

Lavery, Brian, *Churchill's Navy: The Ships, Men and Organisation 1939–45*, Conway Maritime Press, London, 2006

Ministry of Information, *The Mediterranean Fleet: Greece to Tripoli – The Admiralty Account of Naval Operations, April 1941 to January 1943*, HMSO, London, 1944

Mizzi, John A., *Operation Pedestal: The story of the Santa Marija Convoy*, Midsea Books, Valletta, 2012

O'Hara, Vincent, *Struggle for the Middle Sea: The Great Navies at War in the Mediterranean 1940–45*, Conway Maritime Press, London, 2009

Pearson, Michael, *The Ohio and Malta: The Legendary Tanker that Refused to Die*, Pen & Sword Maritime, Barnsley, 2004

Preston, Anthony (ed.), *Jane's Fighting Ships of World War II*, Bracken Books, London, 1989 (originally published by Jane's Publishing Company, London, 1947)

Roberts, John, *British Warships of the Second World War*, Seaforth Publishing, Barnsley, 2017

Roskill, Stephen W., *The War at Sea*, Vol. 3, Part 1 (History of the Second World War series), HM Stationery Office, London, 1954

Sadkovitch, James, *The Italian Navy in World War II*, Praeger Publishing, Santa Barbara, CA, 1994

Smith, Peter C., *Pedestal: The Malta Convoy of August 1942*, William Kimber Ltd., London, 1987

Smith, Peter C., *Stukas over the Mediterranean 1940–45*, Greenhill Books, London, 1999

Woodman, Richard, *Malta Convoys, 1940–1943*, John Murray, London, 2000

INDEX

Figures in **bold** refer to illustrations and captions.